Ripe

HARVESTING the VALUE
OF YOUR BUSINESS

Deborah Douglas

SelectBooks, Inc.
New York

This edition published by SelectBooks, Inc.
For information address SelectBooks, Inc., New York, New York.

First Edition

ISBN 978-1-59079-193-6

Library of Congress Cataloging-in-Publication Data

Douglas, Deborah L.
  Ripe : harvesting the value of your business / Deborah Douglas. -- 1st ed.
    p. cm.
  Includes index.
  Summary: "Presents information about how to prepare a privately held business for a sale, and how to conduct the selling process for optimal profit"--Provided by publisher.
  ISBN 978-1-59079-193-6 (hbk. : alk. paper)
  1. Sale of business enterprises. 2. Business enterprises--Valuation. I. Title.
HD1393.25.D67 2009
658.1′64--dc22
                                    2009005227

Interior text design by Janice Benight

Manufactured in the United States of America

10 9 8 7 6 5 4 3 2 1

DEDICATION

For Richard, Mom and Dad, and Juli—
the essence of love, family, and friendship

Preface

WE HAVE RECENTLY experienced one of the most turbulent financial periods of a lifetime for most Americans as we have endured the pain of a truly great recession. When we finally emerge from this to enter the next economic cycle, successful business owners will have tremendous opportunities to harvest their reward for building private businesses that have stood the test of these tough times. With the overall economy on the precipice of recovery, would-be sellers will soon have the opportunity to cash in on a lifetime of hard work. Today, many are now ready, and are eagerly looking forward to the right time to reap the incredible financial benefits possible from sale.

Private company owners, who only a few years ago were "close" to considering an exit, found their efforts delayed by a dismal economy. In 2009 when the economy was turbulent, many owners were hanging on for dear life, hoping to ride out the storm. Within the next few years, as the world economy steadies (which it will, inevitably) the market for mid-sized business ownership is going to **soar**. Those companies ready and "ripe" will fulfill the dreams, goals, and ambitions of their operators and investors, perhaps like never before.

The Exit Planning Institute predicts that over the next fifteen years, eight million business owners will exit their businesses. Some will pass quietly into the night, as big competitors, and newly emerging king-pins take over. The best of the best will become the building blocks of the future, and their owners will exit with enormous prosperity, while happy and successful next generation managers go on to take those enterprises to new heights

Today the baby-boomer generation is a dominant investing force. People of this generation have pulled their equity of out of the stock market, due to its remarkable instability, and are searching for solid and stable investment opportunities. In the future investors will pursue successful companies that understand the key principles of strategic development and that have been able to produce sustainable and lasting "value."

The legitimate purpose of a business enterprise is to produce wealth, financial security, and increased freedom for its owners. Every owner hopes to at least have the opportunity one day to cash in on their hard work, innovation, and expertise. While there are millions of privately held businesses all over the world, there are many who have almost no idea of how to bring their enterprise to the stage of "ripe" necessary to achieve these goals.

In many years of representing middle market sellers, I have long thought that we could increase the value of each and every client by 25–50%—just by having a few years of knowing them in order to assess the trends and the bends in their particular business direction, and help them to plan, guide, and nourish their enterprises to make them ready for the next phases of growth and success.

The principles, wisdom, and easy-to-relate-to stories within these chapters will give business owners the tools and insights to fortify their companies for success. Whether you plan to sell your business to an investor, transfer ownership to family, or retain your asset indefinitely, you will gain financially from applying the lessons taught and tools shared within this book.

I hope *Ripe* will help owners to do what they need to do—NOW—on the threshold of great economic recovery, to win big for the future.

Acknowledgments

WHEN I THINK OF who gave me what was needed to write this book, I quickly think of my clients. I respect and admire the hard-working business geniuses who I have had the privilege to work with, and I am so grateful for the vast amount I have learned from them, and for the immensely rewarding experiences attained while standing by their sides, during business sale. These are the true builders of the knowledge base that identifies "ripe."

Bill Davenport Sr. and Jr. showed me how a dad and son could put their heads together, and build a magnificent enterprise with value to nourish a family for a lifetime. Thanks to them, and to their wife and Mom Dee, who was the classic supporter with nourishment for both business and family.

Joe Stohldrier, Jennifer Hill, Steve Hoffman, and Gary Ross led a committed group of employee owners to a lifetime home run sale. Their teamwork, in spite of vast differences in personal style and perspective, and their consistent bond and devotion to always doing the right thing for their employee ownership group, was great to be a part of.

Nassim Bayat, Omid Kanini, Jason Farhadi, and Ali Montazeri built and led an amazing and dynamic team of people to a powerful value proposition, in an amazingly short time. It was exciting to watch this company grow and flourish, and to participate with helping their post-sale transitions. Once again, personal integrity pays—for both buyer and seller.

Rob Ashford was the epitome of the classic American entrepreneur, growing one fundamental good concept to a product marketing venture of great proportions—through the purity of hard work, creative energy, and entrepreneurial genius. Rob's mastery of a vast array of consumer product market and control issues, was amazing to watch and learn from.

Art Delis crafted quality performance with a resilient business structure, dealing for decades with hard-to-manage customer dependency issues, and using fundamentals of integrity and a true sense of family among his people, to build his enterprise, as they worked together.

Joe Helmsing found and nourished truly outstanding second tier managers within his organization. Joe's "eye" for talent, and his ability to maximize their contributions to a creative and dynamic corporation, were great to behold.

I could name fifty more clients that I am so grateful for, for the special glimpses they gave me into the very souls of their businesses. To all of my clients—my heartfelt thanks. Your stories abound in this book, and I thank you for your many contributions.

CONTENTS

CHAPTER 3 Tricks of the Trade   89

CHAPTER 4 Negotiating Techniques   135

CHAPTER 1

Coming to Ripe

Ripe

BUSINESS OWNERS OFTEN wonder how they can identify the ideal time for their company to be truly "ripe" for sale. If they miss it, they may miss a once-in-a-lifetime opportunity to create the consummate finale to decades of grueling hard work. Most owners have one chance—and only one—to optimally cash in on that "ripe" moment.

Owners invest time, money, and life force into growing and nurturing their companies. They do so with the intent to promote strong, positive, free economic entities, which will support their families, nourish the families of their workers, and devise ever-improving solutions to the problems and the needs of their customers.

At some point in the progression of development of these companies, the companies grow beyond the natural talents and financial means of the original owners to sustain them. There are hard bumps and turns on the road ahead, which will *require* ever widening resources to successfully navigate.

Companies reaching those thresholds are **RIPE** for transition to the next phase in their development, for finding that next layer of talent and capital to allow them to continue to flourish.

The privately held mid-sized company owner needs to target this level—the level of "ripe"—to win the ultimate reward of financial security for himself and his family, and to help the company he has built to continue moving on it's path toward solidity and prosperity.

This book is about how to build that kind of value. It's about how to recognize when the time has come to consider transition. It's also about "how to" accomplish that transition with maximum financial success, and with maximum potential for long-term ongoing sustenance of the budding company.

Author's Bias: Reward Earned!

There are literally millions of mid-sized, privately owned companies in the world today that have grown from the tiny, one-man idea or talent to become real, emerging forces in the world of business today.

In almost every instance of such "emerging" companies, there was early-stage effort that required twelve hour days, scraping together of hard-fought early stage capital, and the acceptance of significant risk on the part of initial owners.

The companies that grow and develop as the result of these stressful and diligent efforts by entrepreneurial owners, do enormous good for the world. They create jobs for diligent and hardworking employees. They support millions of families. They solve problems for customers. They create life-enhancing products for people around the world. They support the governments for their own nations and others with tax dollars at each point they touch.

All of this early-stage sweat equity and work deserves the payoff the owner/developer can achieve as he or she grows that entity to its next stage, and transitions the "ripe" company to newer, bigger entities to carry on and continue growth.

This book is written from the fundamental perspective and belief that what emerging businesses do for the world is a very good thing. It is written from the foundational premise that profit is a clear, crisp, clean motive, and that such a motive is healthy and good. It both nurtures the growing business entity and motivates owners to invest capital, work hard, and take risks.

As developing businesses do good things for the world, surely we don't want to allow them to die or to atrophy from weaker or less capable ownership at the end of a founder's tenure.

This book is about how to make real business "ripe" for growth, how to harvest the resulting reward for your family, and how to posture your business for success far beyond your personal tenure as CEO.

Own a Company—Not a Job

AUTHOR AND SPEAKER Michael Gerber, perhaps most famous originally for his writing of *The E-Myth*, is a favorite of mine. *The E-Myth*
is an insightful exploration of entrepreneurialism, with fascinating
observations about the personality traits common and even necessary
to the successful business builder. Gerber challenges entrepreneurs
to keep in mind the purpose of building a business, and not to lose
focus on the ultimate objective.

I've enjoyed all of Gerber's books, but after reading the first two I
had the pleasure of hearing him speak. At the outset of his talk, he
looked at the audience with great intensity, and he shouted. "**The only
purpose in this world to own a company is to SELL IT! If you can't
sell it, you don't own a business—you own a JOB!**"

Naturally, as a highly paid expert in the sale of businesses, I like
that thought. However, he is not telling all business owners that they
should sell their companies tomorrow. He is saying is that as long as
your business relies on you, as a worker, to produce income, it's not a
freestanding asset with substantive value. It is, instead, a glorified job.

Admittedly the amount of "glory" in business ownership is highly
questionable. If you want fame, become a rock star, an athlete, or
a politician.

For most entrepreneurs the top priority is not fame or glory.
Typically the entrepreneur seeks independence and financial success.
Neither of those things is ever maximized until the company is able
to "live" without daily owner maintenance.

When you DO sell your company, if you have managed to build
a real productive asset, you will realize many times more benefit when
cashing in. When the company you have built can produce sales,
recruit and retain talented people, and consistently deliver quality
products or services without your personal hands-on touch, you
have created value. You have added to the economic well being of
your community. You have also freed yourself. Great work!

Regardless of when or how you may choose to cash in on the value that you build, remember that your company isn't "done" until it's a living, breathing entity that is self-sustaining.

> *Some years ago as a young CPA, my firm represented a man who owned a thriving mid-sized company with about $30 million in annual sales. The owner received an unsolicited offer to purchase the company for $40 million dollars in cash, with the request for a one-year contract for employment, during which time the new owner could transition management to a replacement CEO. The owner passed on the offer, because he thought that he might want to continue working for up to three to five more years, and he worried that a one-year time frame might be too limiting. Fourteen months after the offer had been made, the owner suffered a stroke. He was out of the office entirely for the next eight months. Production problems surfaced. Sales staff became frustrated with product failures, and distracted with worries about who might emerge as the new CEO. Good people began leaving. By the time the owner returned (even then, only on a part time basis), sales had dropped to around $12 million per year (less than half of the pre-stroke volume), and the company was losing money at an astounding pace. After six months back at work, still fighting health problems and finding it extremely taxing to try to rebuild, the owner decided to sell. Unfortunately, the company was no longer desirable. Enterprise value, as a multiple of earnings, had gone from $40 million to zero. The owner sold assets, liquidated the corporation, and barely cleared enough to cover debt. His $40 million in value was lost, all because he was worried about keeping his job.*

Don't fall into the trap of "I'm old enough, I've worked hard, and the world owes me a living." It doesn't. *It was here first.*

Build your company, make it strong, and create value! Ownership of a saleable company is the ultimate job security.

The Benefit of the Niche

MOST BUSINESS OWNERS begin with a vision. They may not really frame it in their mind as a "vision," but nonetheless, they have one. At the core, the vision begins with some void or weakness in the marketplace, which the aspiring new owner thinks he can competitively fill with a new product or service.

> *Rock Sathre started a manufacturing company in a small rented garage. He manufactured custom subassemblies for various customers. He made his own tooling, designed to enhance production quality and to solve special problems for his customers. He knew he could provide competitive services because he could solve certain types of manufacturing problems that others couldn't. Industrial Custom Products was formed.*
>
> *Nancy Friedman complained to her insurance agent about his horrible telephone reception and service. At his request she came in a week later and spent an hour telling his staff how to do a better job in responding to customers on the phone. Results were so good that she then had several follow up calls from friends of his, asking her to do the same for their companies. It didn't take long for her to say, "This is a need in the marketplace which I can fill." Her company, called Telephone Doctor, was formed.*

The initial vision for a business is generally a focused concept for filling a needed niche. Over time, this initial clarity of the enterprise vision naturally changes and evolves. Opportunities come along which, although not the original focus of the business, seem to offer short-term help to building revenue levels. The owner tells himself he's "expanding" into other areas. The incidental new business that happens along is happily folded in as increased revenue, without much scrutiny as to its relative fit with the initial concept. Focus becomes blurred.

These are natural responses to normal patterns of growth and evolution. Unfortunately these "natural" patterns can be dangerous. Growth without focus can be hazardous to your company's health.

Strategic buyers—the ones who pay most dearly for the select enterprises that they want—search for FOCUS. They want the niche player who has carved out a special spot, where he is king.

So what is a "niche"? What does that really mean in form and appearance?

For the manufacturer it may mean that you are the only provider of a patented technology or a "family" of patented technologies. For a distributor it may mean that you are THE supplier of 70% of a narrow given category of product in the U.S. For a service company it may mean a solid reputation as the best provider of a single service. For a retailer it may mean you have the most complete stock within a particular well-defined product category.

It may be a focus on customers whom you understand, an extended service capability that perfectly fills a need, or an element of quality that you alone have perfected.

Aristotle Onassis said the secret of all business is to know something that nobody else knows. That advantage is what gives you focus.

When buyers see it, they want it. Your margins of profit are higher than others because of your niche position. Your competition will have far greater trouble displacing you. You have the momentum of success in one focused area, which is likely to build naturally upon itself and multiply, in continuation of a solid trend line.

In the entire world of attributes that add value to businesses, there is no one element as important as FOCUS.

"Put all of your eggs in one basket—then watch the basket."
—MARK TWAIN

We represented the owner of a plastic manufacturing company who was eager to sell his business, and who was very excited about his niche. He informed me that he had not only one, but TWO niches! Even better than one! His company was a leading manufacturer of every plastic part imaginable for the snowmobile industry, from fenders to dash panels to mirror trim. They had the best clients in the world in this segment, and they proudly strived to know more than anyone in the world about snowmobile production issues, market demand, and even timing for their customers' production needs.

At the same time, the company was also fast becoming one of the top producers of antistatic packaging in the U.S. These two markets accounted for around 80% of the company's business and the other 20% was somewhat ad hoc. Ad hoc in this case did not mean unimportant. The company cared meticulously for all of its customers, and had many special little pet products. As a result, profits were great, customer relationships were excellent, and we were thrilled to take this fine company to market.

We researched and probed and carefully screened to identify the "best" prospective buyers. Packaging concerns were paying great prices for acquisitions. Our client sold antistatic packaging products to the computer and telecommunications giants, and the major players in this market were cool and polished developers of the mega-sized customer account. They recognized promising value in our client, particularly in one clever product design, and in its niche development of budding new antistatic solutions. Thus they found the company very interesting. However, when viewed in total, one after another concluded that it was not quite a natural fit. "We love the antistatic packaging niche these people have carved out, and it could be a great complement to our other product offerings. But ... is that a snowmobile fender?"

The recreational vehicle types were a hardier, more free-wheeling crowd, with great appreciation for our client's understanding of their customers. "These guys really know their stuff. Look at these ingenious hand guards that won't break—even at 100 degrees below! But what in the world are those antistatic people doing? Production people wearing hairnets and booties really seem a little outside of our range."

The two business segments couldn't be split apart because they shared too many people, too much capital equipment base, and all of their space. The company was still great, and commanded a good price, but if either one of the segments alone had represented a vast share of the business, the company would probably have brought at least 25% more, as a multiple of earnings.

Is there risk in focus? Sure. But it creates power and life and targeted drive, which is usually worth the risk.

As one of my Texan clients once put it, "If you're gonna be great, you gotta figure out where you're goin', and you gotta commit. There's nothin' in the middle of the road but yellow stripes and dead armadillos."

Building Second Tier

A company is known by the people it keeps.

THE BUILDERS OF COMPANIES are often entrepreneurial geniuses who work very hard in every aspect of their business. They tend to find that it's hard to get employees who care as much as they do about the outcome of their business performance. Often they find it easier to keep the ultimate control in their own capable hands, because it is so difficult to develop managers within, able to do an equally skilled job.

As far back as 1720 Voltaire observed "it's not the scarcity of money, but the scarcity of men and talents, which constrains success." Outstanding people are hard to find.

Buyers want companies with in-house talent adequate to sustain the business, even if the owner, post sale, decides to retire or work far less. After sale, buyers don't really expect the owner's interest to be as strong as it was before. The owner will no longer be dependent upon the business for his principal personal net worth, as he was before sale.

We see certain traumatic volume thresholds in business development which are standard pressure points resulting from budding needs that come with growth. The talent and capabilities of second tier management increase predictably at certain volume thresholds. For example, the $10 million level, and again the $50 million level, seem to be frequent points of trauma.

At around $10 million in volume the owner first comes head to head with the powerful need for a real second-tier management group. The enterprise is simply too large for one owner to do it all by himself. Often the areas most loved by the founding owner are the ones easiest for him to replace first. The natural-born engineer will more easily develop great engineering talent than sales skill or human resource talents. The gifted salesman has an innate ability to identify sales talent, and to teach sales management skills. Because the owner is often at ease with people and naturally skilled at helping people to develop their own skills, the owner often finds himself most easily transitioning away from his strong points. Soon he may be left with greatest responsibility only for those areas that he dislikes. Thus he finds himself working excessively hard, in functions that he finds increasingly unpleasant. Bad combination.

Developing and keeping second-tier talent is a basic requirement in the quest for achieving value. Test and probe skills, nurture talent, and gradually encourage and increase employees' responsibilities to develop management skills. Seek to insure that customer relationships are wide and deep, and do not become vested in solitary individuals (including yourself). Establish early policies requiring noncompete agreements for important positions. Look for opportunities to advance people who are good at developing even more talent at the next lower tier. Focus on development for the longer-term future, to prepare for the next wave of growth.

Remember, the only thing worse than training employees and losing them is not training employees and keeping them. Take the time to develop management talent in your organization, and then loosen the reins enough to allow them to flourish.

The more your business is self-sustaining and able to operate profitably and well without your personal time and attention, the better its value will be. Also, the side benefit (not insignificant) is greater personal flexibility for you and greater durability in times of crisis for your company. It pays to work yourself out of a job.

Safety & Compliance

AS BUYERS APPROACH purchase of a company, they are naturally very interested in and concerned about the company's safety history, the history of compliance with labor safety rules, environmental laws, and every kind of regulated compliance issue. A fault in the historical compliance trail could mean later exposure for a new owner from governing authorities. The bigger and stronger the buyer, the more stringent they are likely to be in scrutiny of such matters. The larger players have, from necessity, come to understand the exposures they face as a "deep pocketed" producer, and they often feel that a culture of carelessness, or inattentiveness to safety and other compliance matters, is very hard to correct.

> *Several years ago our firm courted an offer from Alcoa to purchase one of our client's major manufacturing operations. The offer was good—and Alcoa could do much good for the long-term future of the company post sale. By way of background, Alcoa had long dealt with a range of environmental and safety issues, and was very attentive and very disciplined in handling such matters to keep company exposures to an absolute minimum.*

When the Alcoa crew visited the site of our client's business operations, they were put off by a number of obvious indicators of inattention to regulatory compliance matters. There were OSHA bulletin boards with notices about safety and changing rules, containing notices that were three to five years old, graying with age and dust, and obviously not updated or attended to for years. There were towers of packaging product that went as high as 10 to 20 feet above any level of support, and some of the towers listed to one side when stacked materials became askew as they were added to the piles. Forklift drivers rushed through the plant, and our guests looked frightened or nervous as the trucks passed by them so rapidly.

After the plant tour the Alcoa M&A directors who had extended the initial offer, and coordinated the visit, came to us and said they would not continue to pursue the acquisition. They said they loved the product, and the company's foothold in a desirable niche for them, but they said they had found that when a large plant of this type fell into bad habits regarding safety and compliance, it was extremely difficult to instill the employees with a healthy respect for those issues. They said they simply could not afford to replace the massive count of supervisory and management people they would likely need to replace, and thus they withdrew their offer.

Owners of manufacturing facilities in particular, frequently do get exhausted with attempting to comply for a long time with all the labor and safety rules. This is often one of the key thorns in the side of owners, one which can cause them to want to sell. We understand this, and we sympathize with their difficulties, but plant conditions can also seriously affect the company's value. In spite of the pain, time, and cost involved, there are many reasons that safety and compliance issues are well worth attending to.

A client business owner recently told us a story, which he said he felt was a bit silly, but sometimes came all too close to the way his management staff felt about compliance matters. He told us a story of a friend who was contemplating an innovative new surgical procedure.

> *The friend had heard that it was now possible to obtain a brain transplant, so he wanted to check it out. He asked his doctor how much such a procedure would cost. The doctor said, "Well ... it really depends on what type of brain you are getting. I can get you a pilot's brain for around $300,000. Or, I could get you a doctor's brain for about $500,000. Or, if you really want to splurge, I could arrange to get you an OSHA inspector's brain—but that one would cost you about $5,000,000." The patient listened, and then squinted in confusion as he took all of this in. He said to his doctor, "Why in the world would the OSHA guy's brain cost such a huge amount more?" The doctor looked at him wisely, and answered, "Well, it's never been used."*

Business owners simply can't afford the indulgence of allowing staff to decide which regulations or rules are really worth complying with. It doesn't matter if you're right or wrong about the quality of or the reasons for the rules—if they are authorized by the law or a defined regulation, they are WORTH the time and effort to obey. Think about each of the following categories if they apply to your organization, and define mechanisms to ensure careful compliance by supporting staff:

- OSHA rules
- Negotiated labor contract rules
- Environmental compliance
- Sewer and water drainage compliance
- Sales and use tax rules and compliance
- Contractor versus employee definitions and compliance
- Air quality and emissions compliance

Careful design of mechanisms to ensure sound trails of compliance will be absolutely necessary, if you hope to court offers for purchase of stock instead of assets (often for a vastly preferable income tax outcome), and may be critical to courting any offer from the well-heeled and powerful larger company.

Employee Solidity

AS BUYERS SEEK to evaluate any acquisition candidate, they will inevitably look pretty carefully at the likelihood of retaining valued employee base, and at the positioning for potential additions of future staff as they grow.

In considering likely retention, they naturally begin with evaluation of key management staffing. As we design materials for presentation to buyers, we seek always to learn everything we can about what makes current mid-level staffing strong or weak. What talents are currently strong within the organization, and how are those people paid? Are there any employment agreements or longer term, upside possibilities built into the comp structure to encourage people to stay? Often our seller-clients will suggest that we "add back" discretionary bonus amounts, with the argument that the company could have made more, had owners not chosen to pay such bonuses. That rarely flies well with buyers, because they want to keep employees, and keep them just as happy as they are today (or more). If they, perhaps for the first time, decide to omit all bonus payments to employees, retention naturally becomes far less likely.

Buyers especially like to know about the upper middle management tier of employees—perhaps the top five to fifteen people within the management group. They want to know age, experience, key skills, and strengths, and they want a clear understanding of current employment commitments such as contracts, noncompete agreements, termination benefits, and bonus expectations.

If key second-tier people are good and worth keeping, emphasize those strengths, and help the buyer figure out ways to encourage and incent them to stay for a long time to come. If there are holes or weaknesses in your second-tier entourage, admit such weaknesses, and let buyers know that this is an area where their help and improvements could be meaningful and very productive for the company.

If you have well-drawn noncompetes in place for important second-tier people, you are far more secure in the eyes of buyers. If you do not have noncompete agreements in place for employees, it is difficult to put them in place immediately prior to sale. You run the risk of either **(a)** employees being unhappy, and choosing to leave the company rather than sign, or **(b)** employees signing and then feeling very much betrayed, if you had them sign without telling them that they risk working for new owners.

We have worked in many situations where the retaining of the number-two key employees was very important in the event of a sale. In some of the cases these important employees have been told of the possible sale, and have been provided with incentive agreements to ensure their cooperation with the selling effort. The benefit to be paid to the key employee might include substantial cash bonus, payable only after reasonable post-sale retention. Usually with any such commitment the employee is also required to maintain confidentiality—with risk of benefit forfeiture if such confidentiality is breached. This is a sensitive and difficult negotiation, and is appropriate only for the most valued and critical of staff.

> *A few years ago, our firm sold a company that was growing rapidly, and which had a handful of very key employees, who were absolutely NEEDED for the company's survival and success as they worked on several major contracts over the coming several years. Our client had hired, trained, and given great care to development of this fine staff, and he wanted to keep them happy and productive post sale. He suggested payment to this key group of a very major bonus (almost 10% of his total very large purchase price), which he wanted to offer at close, as a way to thank them*

for their great work. The buyers were extremely negative about this concept, because they felt that this would give every top-level person enough financial "cushion" to feel very comfortable quitting to search for a new employer. The two ended up compromising, with the seller setting aside his desired bonus amount in an escrow account, which the key people would receive as bonus over a three-year period post sale if they stayed with the company. The bonuses were paid as planned, and every one of the key people stayed through that time. This left the buyers with enough time to win the hearts of their new employees, and yet still allowed our seller to reward people as he had intended. This was a fine win/win solution for all parties to the transaction.

Buyers will want all possible information on pending union agreements, and histories of past union negotiations. Some buyers have absolute preferences about union or non-union workforces, and this may definitely take some buyers out of the running entirely, if you don't fit their preferred profile. Buyers also will seek information on where new additions to your workforce are likely to come from, and how plentiful such people are likely to be in your area. Are there colleges and universities to support new young people in the areas of expertise you may need? Is the population growing and/or adequate to supply new trainees in your market area?

The more solid information you can build into your company profile to demonstrate accessibility to quality new workforce, the stronger your company will appear to interested buyers.

Facility & Equipment Issues

THERE CAN BE a natural tendency on the part of an owner thinking about a possible sale to be reluctant or hesitant to invest significant capital in the business for the period of a few months, or even a few years, before he sells. This is a normal reluctance, because "pay-back" or a future benefit for such an investment may not happen, because he will have sold his business.

Buyers worry about such tendencies and will look hard at the operation to assess any possible accumulation of capital needs that may result. Normally buyers will ask to see a history of capital expenditures back to perhaps five to ten years before sale. Most sound businesses require some base of ongoing level of capital expenditure to remain healthy.

Typically as buyers study historic cash flow for the business, they will look at pretax income, add back depreciation and interest expense (to get to EBITDA—earnings before interest, taxes, and depreciation allowance), and then they will deduct from that the capital expenditures for each year, in order to really get to a cash flow number.

The more solid, sturdy, and well-planned capital issues are, the better the perception for sale.

If equipment is old and outdated, especially if there is a big decrease in spending or in maintenance in recent years, buyers will be likely to figure this into value calculations. On the other hand, if capital spending has run unusually high in recent years, for things that offer significant long-term benefit, this may actually be a "plus" for value.

Sellers need to prepare a long-term assessment of CapX (Capital Expenditures) over the past five to ten years before sale, and be prepared to answer questions about significant changes. They also need to prepare a wish-list for potential improvements that they are considering, and a plan for which such improvements may be advisable in the near-term, along with estimates for "payback" of such improvements.

Capital improvements, which significantly enhance abilities to support increased sales, or to reduce costs and thus improve margins immediately, are often well received by buyers. However, improvements which are perceived as "catch-up" items—those items needed simply to stay afloat—will detract from value.

Some years ago we sold an injection molding manufacturer, which had a history of capital expenditures of almost one million dollars per year for a ten-year period prior to sale. For the three years immediately prior to sale, however, such CapX had dropped to 200,000 to 250,000 dollars per year. Fortunately, we were able to stir excellent competition for the deal, and still get very strong offers. Our winning bidder shared with us their value analysis. They had bid 18 million dollars for the transaction, on a company with net pretax cash flow of slightly under 3 million dollars. We tallied this to be approximately a six multiple on cash flow. The buyer, however, said that they had tallied their bid at a full seven multiple. Seven times their 3 million dollar cash flow would have been 21 million dollars for the sale. However, that buyer then deducted from their 21 million value a 3 million dollar "capital catch up" factor in their valuation, because they feared that the company had been neglecting needed replacements in recent years. Thus the bid was 18 million dollars net. This bid was still stronger than others, and won the day.

If capital expenditures are for long-term assets, which can be expected to benefit the company for years to come, buyers may consider that an add-back to value.

We sold a company last year, which had just invested 5 million dollars in a new building. Buyers, almost universally, did not consider that capital expenditure to be a reduction to cash flow as they assessed the value. It was clear the benefits of the new building would have substantial payoff for years to come, and virtually none of that payoff had yet boosted earnings (In fact, the cost of moving into the new facility—most of which was operating expense and not capitalized—was generally perceived as a valid add-back to the year's earnings.)

A healthy study of CapX histories and potential CapX needs, along with likely pay-back, is very helpful as any company approaches sale.

Additionally, this is a very healthy ongoing business practice for controlling and keeping tabs on capital needs, in any company.

Family Matters

BUSINESS OWNERS OFTEN torment themselves about family succession issues. They have a natural desire to give their children a "head start" in life. The owner wants to let his children pick up at the summit of what he has accomplished.

There is no more natural desire for a parent. However, beware of the pitfalls.

Second generation business people often do not have the talent or skills to pick up in the next stage of the business evolution. It's very difficult to build entrepreneurial instincts into a child growing up as son of the boss. If they don't have the raw capability, you will harm both their psyche and their inheritance by putting them in a position to ultimately fail.

> *As you plan for business ownership transition, keep in mind that kids working in the business view things quite differently from the kids outside of the business. Family ownership can be an enormous source of sibling conflict. The kids in the business will think, "I helped to build this business. I was toiling away for all of these years, and I have earned a greater reward than my siblings outside." The kids not in the business, in response will think, "You had a job given to you for all of those years. You got the company car and the benefits. I, on the other hand, had to make my own way in the world. You have had disproportionate advantages."*

If you think it's complicated to contemplate sale with one set of family members ... that's a day in the park in comparison to the third or later generations, with multiple family units involved. If you have more than one family member involved, and there are likely to be multiple kids as heirs, develop a mechanism now to shift control to one or two key operators. Do not leave it to be decided and agreed by those increasingly diverse next generation beneficiaries.

> *We did some expert witness testimony for a family where three siblings worked in the business, and several third generation kids were employed by the company as well. As the years passed the family segmented into two factions, dramatically at odds. One wanted to sell and one did not. The non-sellers obstructed sale in every way possible. The bitterness and unreasonableness on the part of both sides was unbelievable.*
>
> *The matter finally went to court, and a judge ruled that a sale was the only possible option. Unfortunately, however, that judgment was late in coming. By that time, the owners of the company had diminished its value to about one-third of its former glory. In the meantime, multiple lawsuits had been filed, a five-generation family vacation property (owned by all) had been sold in a fit of rage by the managing trustee, and a competitive business had been formed by two of the third generation kids. The family relationship was destroyed, and the value of the business with it.*

Family ownership transition is risky business. Think twice about your priorities before you give a gift or "sell" to a child, and think ten times before you sell to more than one.

Also, business owners need to realize that selling a business with multiple siblings active and involved in the company can be very tricky. Buyers will be forced to choose the future promotions and determine employment success for those family members remaining active in the business. If they promote one instead of another, they face potential ill-will from siblings. Family loyalties can make it extremely awkward for some to stay and thrive, while others are ushered out.

> *We were hired by a prospective client to estimate likelihood of salable value for a little company with about $10 million in sales, which had several family members very involved in the business.*

Actually, there were five sons of the owner actively employed by the company, and three of those five thought they were likely candidates to be the successor to Dad and the future CEO. Dad maintained the role as CEO, but he had health problems, and clearly was going to need to move top-level responsibility to a successor in the not-too-distant future. We advised Dad to either choose a son to be a successor at that time or to hire an outside third party to step into the CEO role. Buyers would not deal well with the "no-one-at-the-top" real life scenario, and every key position in the company was occupied by a very intimate family member.

Gathering Market Intelligence

ONE EXTREMELY USEFUL element in preparation for sale, which can and should be practiced well in advance of sale, is the gathering of market intelligence. Such intelligence includes data about who the buyers commonly are in your business segment, but it's also much more. It's about how buyers determine value, and what types of companies they like to buy. Discovering long-term trends and patterns in your industry can be immensely helpful when it's time to cash in. Additionally, the accumulation of operating statistical information about others in your industry can be a great tool. It will alert you to problems and opportunities, whether you're considering sale or not. Finally, when the time comes to sell, it gives you powerful ammunition with which to identify and better prove your strengths by comparison to industry norms.

Many business owners think they are gathering intelligent merger/acquisition data simply by dropping into a file the letters of people who write to them with potential interest. First of all, 90% of those letters come from business brokers, investment fund buyers and displaced executives who are would-be buyers. These are not the most credible or focused contenders for optimum purchase. Secondly, even letters from viable suitors who are in the market and who really do know who you are and what you do, are of fleeting value. Buyers who really have intent and determination to buy usually make their move within a year or less. Either they get several deals done, after which they are "full" for a time, or they progress further in their study of what they want to buy, and their prime targets evolve.

The process of gathering functionally useful market intelligence is best pursued from several different angles. You need to find out:

(1) who is buying whom, what are they paying for purchase and what are their long-term strategic targets,

(2) what is average and what is good performance in your business niche, and how do you measure in comparison to others in your market, and

(3) what are the long-term trends and shifts taking place in your industry, with respect to the basic shape and form of your prime customers, your product and its delivery?

With respect to the first item—who is acquiring—owners often hear of sale transactions in their industry soon after they happen. However, gathering true information on the details about pricing and other critical elements to the deal may be far more difficult. If you know the buyer or the seller personally—ask. If you don't know them personally, but you have the courage to call, or if a chance encounter brings you in touch—ask. Ask what was paid, and what form that payment took. Did they pay with cash, stock, notes payable, or what type of consideration? Was payment made in full at closing, or was some portion of the payment deferred? Did they buy assets only or did they assume liabilities too? Was the seller required to pay down debt with the proceeds from sale?

Were there multiple bidders for the company? If so, whom? Naturally, only the closest of friends or the most distant of acquaintances will answer this wide range of questions openly. However, learn what you can, and take notes. File the information away because you will someday find it very useful data!

The second bucket of intelligence to gather relates to statistical industry norms. In some industries an owner can gather excellent data of this type directly from trade associations and magazines. More commonly, however, the information which is publicly available is imprecise and not very on-point to the actual business in question. For example, industry categories are often too broad to allow accurate comparisons. Obtain all possible information, but don't use it without careful scrutiny.

Mark Twain said, *"There are three kinds of lies:* **(1)** *lies,* **(2)** *damned lies, and* **(3)** *statistics."* Statistical comparisons are worth the time to obtain and analyze, but only with due care to find information of real pertinence and comparability.

The better segmented and more specific the data, the better. The best information may come from buying groups or joint venture alliances, or even from conversations with friends. The more you are able to build your understanding of how you fit into the picture of your total market, and where your company is particularly strong or weak, the better you will be able to deal with the questions that will arise in marketing your company.

The third segment of intelligence relates to the big picture. What are the important, sweeping changes coming to your industry segment? The moment you cease glancing up at the horizon to ensure that your direction is true and your progress is steady, you endanger your company's future.

Philip Wrigley, Chairman of the great Chicago-based Wrigley Gum Company, was once interviewed by a reporter on a long trans-Atlantic flight. The reporter asked why he traveled tens of thousands of miles every year to personally visit each major market in which the company's product sold. Wrigley quickly replied, "For the same reason the pilot of this plane keeps the engine running when we're already twenty-nine thousand feet up."

It pays to remain vigilant and attentive to changes in your market-place. If you were an automotive parts warehouse distributor in the 1980s with good future vision, you got out. You realized that this entire layer of the distribution network was heading toward obsolescence.

If you were a conveyor fabricator in the 1990s, you may have seen a great opportunity coming from a veritable explosion in the sophistication of warehouse systems. If you saw and appreciated the changes to come, you may well have begun to develop specialized competency to fit this evolving market. If you did so you probably doubled your business value very quickly.

> *In the 1980s, smart automotive warehouse distributors sold to the retail chains, which were taking over their entire layer of business function. In the 1990s, conveyor manufacturers combined with system integrators, software designers, and design/build manufacturers focusing on enormous and complex facilities. These were the paths to very fast maximization of wealth for such business owners*

The big picture elements are the gradual but significant trends. They may be trends for providers to offer a greater range of service. They may be tendencies toward increasing specialization. Unfortunately, the more difficult any business is to operate, or the more stressed the operation becomes, the less likely the owner is to distance himself adequately to really examine the trends. When business is tough, most owners tend to buckle down, and focus on the details with such intensity that they totally lose sight of the big picture.

> *Some years ago we sold a boat manufacturer owned by a single individual, who was also the CEO. Early in the "getting acquainted" stages, he became completely unavailable for several days, while he attended a company planning retreat. Upon his return we asked how the retreat went and if his team was successfully fired up for another good year. He corrected our misconception and explained that he took his planning retreat all*

alone—just to personally spend time in focus upon where he was and where he was going. He was a tremendously successful business operator, and I'm convinced that his annual retreat helped.

Once every few months the prudent owner will lift his head and try to look from afar. Such vision will offer keen insights not only into prudent operating or marketing direction, but also into sourcing for premium buyers of the future.

Timing Your Move

OWNERS HAVE A TENDENCY to contemplate a sale when they are nervous or tired or both. Naturally, it's most tempting to exit when you're less than pumped up about your future. When two semi-major disasters have fallen from the sky, and sixteen more have threatened, one begins to think about getting out while the getting's good. The ever-present risk of business ownership begins to weigh heavily.

In the immortal words of one of our clients: "Every time I think I'm winning the rat race ... along comes a faster rat!"

When is the best time to sell in order to maximize value? Of course, it's just before you get to the top of the hill. It's just after the best string of good times the company has ever had. It's the year of the best success ever.

Part of the timing issue revolves around the economic prognosis. Most business owners wouldn't even pretend to be great economic gurus. I once heard Federal Reserve Chairman Alan Greenspan, speaking to a group of business owners. In his introductory remarks, he said, *"I guess I should warn you: if I turn out to be particularly clear, you've probably misunderstood what I've said."* The economy is complex and almost impossible to forecast reliably. However, most business owners do tend to have a fairly reliable instinct for the short-term future of their own business niche.

For the long, stable, growing operation, the "best time" may be hard to anticipate. Although the clear objective is to sell just before any downturn, it's difficult to predict when a downturn will come. However, any reasonably strong recent history will serve you well and pay off. Buyers generally will feel they should pay a multiple of the last running twelve months of profits. If you've been down-turning for the past two years, but you're hoping they'll pay for an average of the past five years' performance, you're kidding yourself. If at the other extreme, your most recent year is a complete oddity, with super performance for the first and only time in history, you will have a credibility issue. This problem is actually not quite as serious, in that a reasonable likelihood of continuation at the new high levels will make buyers dismiss the bygone lackluster years as irrelevant. However, buyers will need to understand enough about your business to believe in the profitable continuation of the upturn.

The business life cycle for the single owner enterprise often runs something like this:

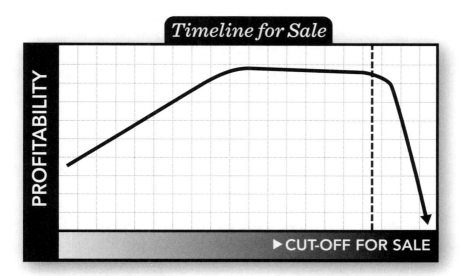

Unfortunately all too many owners delay action on a possible sale until the last possible moment, when they've come too close to falling off the cliff. They know they should sell, and they know that value is declining, but they're afraid to make their move. They procrastinate due to fear that perhaps it's too soon to give up and they cling to unrealistic hope for the magical comeback.

> *My teenaged son was a wrestler. One of the young men on his team suffered losses repeatedly and painfully. After one particularly disheartening match, we saw the assistant coach give the youngster twenty minutes of pep talk to cheer and to encourage him. It was between rounds, and the kids were taking a break, so my son sat beside his father and me, and observed the pep talk. Afterward, he shook his head slowly, and said, "What if, right at this very moment, he is already living up to his full potential?"*

There have been times when I thought that words to similar effect might be the kindest revelation I could make to a particularly struggling perspective client. If you find yourself running a company on a downhill track, do yourself a favor by recognizing the issue, and taking decisive action. Sell before the downhill slope becomes too steep.

Advice from one of our sage clients: *"Eat right. Exercise. Die anyway."* Life is too short.

There is a time in the life of every problem when it's big enough to see, but small enough to solve. Move, then.

Another common misstep we see in timing involves the company that has a new high-tech product about to unfold. Biotech and information technology companies often face this position. The best moment for sale in this environment is inevitably after proof of viability and function, but BEFORE the attempt to go full force with the new product to the broad market. These companies are actually the most sensitive and volatile of all with respect to timing for sale. The promise or the hope of enormous success is often far more valuable than the final outcome. Buyers will bid for the chance to own a hit.

The upstart development company which is great at managing through the creative torment of early product innovation is rarely capable of the rigorous business discipline required in taking a fast evolving product to market maturity. Also, in almost every case of innovative product development, time is of the essence. Even with patent protections, competitors will look for ways to introduce similar products. Some may even trounce directly on proprietary patent rights, and dare the developer to spend the time and money to try to stop them. Regardless of how it may come to pass, expect competitive energy to surface quickly around any successful new product.

Some years ago our firm worked with a healthcare company that had developed an outstanding new product with a truly remarkable drug delivery system. The product was in FDA approval testing, and initial results were extremely promising. Additionally, because the product involved a new and innovative subcutaneous drug delivery mechanism, which allowed for time-released medication, the potential for the product (in terms of possible expansion to other new pharmaceutical products) was enormous. The owners of the company had about $4 million invested, from their own hard-earned money, in developing the product to reach this stage.

In our first stage inquires about the product, we had a very quick offer of $15 million for the product rights. The owners decided that this was not enough—because eventually they hoped it could be a $100 million product value. We had hopes that we might get continuing and growing appetite for the product, as we courted other buyers, but our client felt the time wasn't right. They declined the open offer, and took the rights off the market.

Six months later, one of the large pharmaceutical companies came up with a similar, but better product. Interest in our client's operation dried up almost entirely, overnight. They closed the operation about six months later, with an aggregate net loss on

the venture of over $6 million. When they thought back to the
$11 million gain they had passed on, they were devastated.

The high-tech developer of new products can make fast profit and avoid enormous risk by courting competitive bids for purchase, just before time for the all-out sales/production effort. Unfortunately however, the inventive, entrepreneurial personality, nurtured with some technological success, can become excessively optimistic. Early-stage developers often don't appreciate the risks and the pitfalls of rapid growth. They think they can sort it out as they go, but in four out of five cases, they fail. It's often worth a sacrifice of half of the ultimate potential, just to avoid the risk of fumble. Instead, consider capitalizing on the eager competitive spirit of those who are the experts in sale and mass production of your type of product. Think carefully before you choose to delay. AFTER full product rollout, buyers are going to expect proof of ultimate potential, in the form of magnificent sales and stunning profits.

If the time for sale is close to right, and you're close to ready, it simply doesn't pay to wait until every star in the heavens is perfectly aligned. Avoid stress and risk. *Let the wind blow through your hair while you still have some!*

CHAPTER 2

The Selling Process

Mechanics of the Sale

THERE ARE A NUMBER of possible approaches to the selling process, and there is probably no fixed, "right" way to ensure success. The selling process described here will focus on the normal mechanisms used by our firm to sell privately held middle market companies. These mechanisms are not rigidly cast in stone, but generally, they do work—and for our firm they have resulted in successfully consummated sale transactions for 95% of the clients we have represented over the past twenty years.

Generally, as we go through the selling process, the main steps and associated timelines for each stage are as follows:

(1) Obtain extensive information on our client seller. Begin development of "core" information exhibits, which buyers will need to assess the opportunity (occurs for the most part between inception of the engagement, and month two or three of the process)

(2) Investigate potential buyers likely to have interest in our seller client. (We normally list, research, and investigate as many as 200–300 potential buyers, and investigate what those buyers want to buy. Our objective is to narrow a top prospect list down to maybe 20 or so. We begin such investigation process immediately after being hired, and continue throughout the engagement, although we often may reach a majority of the initial targets within the first two to three months.)

(3) Obtain signed nondisclosures, and begin sharing specific client information with chosen prospective buyers. (We spend perhaps 30–60 days exchanging first stage information with prospective buyers who we think are likely to be strong fits for our clients.)

(4) Request letter of interest from likely buyers after they have seen strong info on our seller client, and have had adequate time to assess potential interest. (Generally, we find ourselves requesting a nonbinding "letter of interest" from favorite potential buyers often at between the five and six-month mark after beginning of the engagement. We usually seek at least ten of such proposals, to help our client understand his market alternatives.)

(5) Invite favorite two to three buyers to visit client site, tour facility, and meet offsite to talk with owners. (This is likely to occur within two to four weeks of receiving letters of interest from buyers.)

(6) Negotiate outline of purchase agreement, and consider possible letter of intent, in advance of final agreement draft by attorneys. (The object here would be to allow negotiation of substantial issues in advance of final selection of favored buyers, and before full legal draft of the definitive purchase agreement. These negotiations would often entail a two to three week discussion process, immediately following plant tours.)

(7) Facilitate buyer's due diligence and completion of financing verification. (Normally due diligence will involve buyers' CPA firm visiting for one to two weeks, environmental advisors doing Phase I review—or more if problems are identified—and legal review of key documents. Such due diligence process usually takes perhaps two months, with contraction to one for highly efficient processes, and expansion to three in a worst case scenario.)

(8) Draft and work through detailed terms for Definitive Purchase Agreement (We normally will be working on this simultaneously as the buyer is doing due diligence. The process typically takes anywhere from one to three weeks of detailed discussion and negotiation to complete.)

(9) Close of transaction; announcement to staff and key business relationships. (Our average closing date for recent past years has been at about eight months after our hire date. Fastest historically has been around three months after we were hired. Slowest has been around one year.)

The following topics will highlight in greater detail what happens at each stage of this process, and will follow with examples of good and bad—and what we have learned that may help you in your own process.

Hiring an Intermediary

AS ANY COMPANY approaches sale, it is highly advisable to consider quality professional help in the process. As you evaluate potential advisors, you need to look for several things:

FOCUS UPON SELLER REPRESENTATION

The merger and acquisition industry is filled with part time/occasional would-be advisors. They may include accountants, attorneys, friends, bankers, industry operational consultants, brokers who frequently work for buyers, and any range of possible consultants. It's a fun and exciting area of business, which tends to attract ready attention from bright, articulate, and often temporarily unemployed people. It has become an industry filled with part time and occasional players.

Part-time and occasional players do not know how to best sell companies. Their exposure is limited, and their allegiance often shifts from seller to buyer, as they find themselves working in the transaction where they may have other relationships with or benefits from the buyer they are talking with.

Many years ago with almost our first transaction for Douglas Group, we worked for a company whose owner was 70 years old and who wanted to sell. His bankers wanted to help. Debt for the company was significant and scary, and the bank was in a high-risk position. One of the banker directors, who was in fact an astute and successful business manager, was suggested to the owner as an outside hire for presidency of the company.

The company hired this man as president, and then began working on sale. The new president wanted to be the buyer, and the bank was thrilled. The president hired a valuation done on the company, and the valuation firm said that due to losses in recent years, and industry competitive pressure, the company was only worth about $500,000. This was a fairly sizable company, at about $30 million in sales, but the situation was pretty frightening, with the history of recent losses.

We advised that the offer was inadequate, and we suggested that the owner continue with efforts to sell. The bank was very negative about the suggestion and encouraged the board (comprised of old, long-time friends of the owner) to reject this advice and sell for the $500,000 dollars proposed by the president.

The owner took our advice instead. In order to do so, he (as sole shareholder) had to completely dismantle his board of directors, and elect termination of all board members, except himself. It was extremely traumatic for both the owner and his long-time friends.

Three months later we closed sale of the company for $3.5 million in cash. It still was a small value for a company that had been worth far more just five years earlier, but $3.5 million in cash, some eighteen years ago, made a vast difference in the life of the selling shareholder. He was very pleased with results.

FEE STRUCTURES WITH STRONG INCENTIVES

It is critical for owners/shareholders to seek representation with an incentive-based fee structure that puts the intermediary's reward in the right place. Seller intermediaries can be very well paid, but should only make the extremely high-end fees and strong compensation if they achieve great results for their clients.

Common fee structures in the business, for larger companies (say 50 million dollars plus) are very often based on the old "Lehman" formula. The Lehman formula pays the seller rep 5% of the first million dollars, 4% of the next million dollars, 3% of the next million dollars, 2% of the next million, and on to a residual 1% for the remainder. Also, in the smaller middle market transaction, it's fairly common to use a "double Lehman" formula. This formula works 10%, 8%, 6%, 4%, down to a residual 2% of proceeds.

For the smaller company (under 10 million dollars in revenues) a business broker often may charge a flat 10% of all sales proceeds. This is very common for small business transactions, and in fact is almost standard for deals with a total net transaction value of a million dollars or less.

Frankly, I have always felt that a declining fee formula was "backwards," relative to where real value is produced. Nor do I like the flat "one percentage for any sale" sort of format. Our firm normally charges a very modest percentage up to a low-end minimum price point, but then seeks significant bonus potential for proceeds above a certain level. We have found that our clients are generally much happier with this arrangement, and in fact are genuinely pleased when, as a result, they have to pay us a bonus.

All of these fee structures as outlined above refer to the total aggregate fee, likely to be due upon closing. In addition to these amounts, however, almost any intermediary with any substantive value or experience will also charge some level of retainer as they are working on sale. Such retainers for middle market companies will typically range anywhere from $30,000 to $100,000. Many firms require the full retainer to be paid upfront. These retainers may seem steep, but the intermediary needs some level of solid commitment from their client, to insure that the seller is serious about facilitating the transaction, all the way through closing, if they are to be willing to invest the very real volume of professional time to really work on the transaction.

Our firm normally breaks retainers up to a monthly amount, payable as the engagement is ongoing, most typically ranging from $5,000 to $15,000 per month. Meanwhile, we are typically putting in anywhere between $25,000 and $50,000 of time per month, at our normal stated hourly billing rates. We feel that a monthly retainer gives the owner better incentive to facilitate progress toward sale as quickly as possible, and creates less burden to the owner at the outset of the engagement.

SEEK STRONG SUCCESS RATES

It is a fair question for any seller to ask an intermediary what sort of success rates they have with the companies they have worked with in the past, towards sale. Furthermore, as you assess the credibility of any would-be representative, ask also for references of other sellers that the firm has worked with. Other sellers of privately held businesses are much like you. They face the same traumas as they manage the selling process, and often they worry about the same kinds of issues. We typically offer the names of almost any seller we have represented to talk to our new clients, if they would like to. We find that past sellers often talk fairly extensively to our new prospective clients, and really help to give them some insight into what the process is all about.

Any credible and quality professional intermediary should offer significant advantage to their seller client. The following are some of the benefits you should expect, and you should try to assess, in selecting a representative:

Experience
An experienced intermediary should offer hard experience in terms of preparation of company information, negotiating skills, design of workable transaction formats, and building of protective mechanisms for their client.

Arms Length View

The competent third party professional should possess the ability to look at the situation as a buyer might look, and make credible assessments for both problems and opportunities

Credibility to Buyer

An investment banking firm with a solid track record will indicate to buyers that you are truly committed to sale, and provides them with a measure of safety and security that you are providing correct information (both helpful elements if they are to move forward more forcefully)

Time Committments

A decent sized and well-established intermediary should offer ability to devote two or three people with full time effort toward the sale, during a compact time period

Internal Confidentiality

Quality professionals should provide the ability to manage 90% of the sales process through the intermediary's office, thus avoiding constant contact and extensive buyer communication with direct calls to the seller/owner

Negotiating Buffer

Utilizing such third party representatives give the seller client time for careful thought and analysis *before* responding to buyer proposals

Peripheral Vision

It is very difficult for the "do-it-yourself" owner to focus on buyer reactions as they discuss sale (such "peripheral vision" is a **huge** advantage in negotiating most effectively)

Competitive Velocity

There is nothing more important than competitive pressure to make buyers gently but consistently aware of the requirement to offer their most aggressive price and terms

Speed

Outside help can greatly enhance the seller's ability to speed the process. Speed increases likelihood of success (with time frames for completion down to perhaps three to nine months, as compared to the "do-it-yourself" seller average of one to two years.)

Greater Sales Price

The seller's job is to buy as cheaply as is possible; only the need to compete will hold pricing steady at a strong price

Any good intermediary should produce a price at least twenty percent higher than what his client might get on their own. The best, in a strong market environment, can produce a price that is two to three times greater overall.

Developing Information to Present to Buyers

FIRST STAGE INFORMATION NEEDED

INITIAL INFORMATION PROVIDED to buyers should include highlights of the nature of the business to be sold, and status of the operating entity. Such descriptions should normally include strengths of the operation, and competitive advantages of the entity, looking forward. Such strengths in particular should highlight proprietary products or services, potential for growth in the markets of particular strength, and other operating advantages, like management or people power, geographic benefits, and any other elements of the operation, which have proven to be especially helpful to growth and/or profitability.

Early stage information also should carefully craft open admissions of weaknesses for the operation. Buyers will discern those weaknesses as they move forward with due diligence in virtually every case—so they simply cannot remain "hidden." Furthermore (and perhaps even more importantly), up front acknowledgment of the operation's weaknesses may well be perceived by buyers as an opportunity for improvement. There is often a sense that, "if the company is making this much in profit today, in **spite** of this weakness—just think how much we will make, prospectively, after we fix this problem!"

> *Our firm represented a plastic injection molder, which sold sporting goods equipment in relatively small market niches. The company could not compete effectively in really large markets, due to the price pressure from much larger offshore suppliers for mass marketed injection molded products. The company had been downsized substantially over about a decade, due to such competition. As a result, they had a plant physically large enough to do perhaps 40 to 50 million dollars in sales, in spite of a current revenue level of only about 15 million dollars. Fair market value for the company assets, if liquidated, was probably 10 million dollars. The company's cash flow was hovering at about 1 million dollars on its 15 million dollars in gross revenue.*
>
> *As we prepared overview information on the company, we were very upfront in describing the markets the company continued to perform well in, but we also acknowledged the relative "oversize" of the operation. We further emphasized the relatively high fair market value of equipment and facilities, and we obtained all possible fair market value estimates in external supporting matter to support such data.*
>
> *A high percentage of buyers who looked at the company were afraid of the modest earnings level, and either declined to proceed, or offered amounts well below our perceived fair market value in the event of liquidation. Most of the offers for this seller came in at between 5 and 8 million dollars. From the eye-view of any of these buyers, they generally felt they were, even at a 5 to 8 million price point, allowing some premium for potential future of liquidation, if that came to be necessary, because their offers*

were in fact several million dollars above the normal four to six times pretax earnings, common in the industry.

We had to probe about 100 potential suitors for this company, to get ten who continued aggressively after overview stage information. Those who kept coming after this open acknowledgement of our weak spots were real and worthwhile buyers. We ended in selling the company for 13 million dollars, almost all cash up front (an excellent result for a seller with one million dollars in cash flow, and a participant in a tough market with heavy off-shore competition.) The final and best buyers for the company were all aggressive, sales-oriented entrepreneurs, who were eager to seek out more of those smaller size markets, which could be best served by a U.S. based manufacturer. They were prepared to find new customers who would value ability to quickly tailor or alter product to fit specialized and changing needs. We ended with about twenty offers at $5 to $8 million, and three offers well over $10 million.

SECOND STAGE "CORE" INFORMATION ON COMPANY

As a seller prepares information to be ready for buyers, it is important to have basic staples, or "core" information for every buyer who proceeds beyond earliest overview stages. Such core information will generally need to include:

Financial data, including:

   • CPA prepared financial statements (audited or reviewed) for the past several year ends

   • Recent interim year to date statements (at least to last completed quarter, with comparable statements from the same date of prior year)

   • Recast financial statements, showing earnings before owner withdrawals and any substantial benefit (perks) of ownership

Staffing information, including:

- Organization chart

- Recaps of resume highlights on key management

- Compensation levels for all people

- Benefit recaps

- Descriptions of any contracted commitments (bonus arrangements, employment agreements or noncompetes, and severance agreements)

Fixed asset recaps, including:

- Description of real-estate holdings (or, if leased, description of lease terms)

- Latest available appraisal of real-estate owned by company (also, FMV of all real-estate leased from related parties)

- Listings of fixed assets and equipment, including the depreciation schedules and, if available, FMV appraisals

- Historical capital expenditure histories for the past several years

- Capital expenditure projections for major additions needed for several years forward

Marketing information, including:

- Description of sales staffing or sales rep structures (including commission or bonus commitments)

- Analysis of significant future opportunities for growth (including products or services newly introduced or to be introduced, and forward prognosis or timing expected for evolution)

- Listing of proprietary products or services, and any patents, trademarks, or special licensing rights expected to impact competitive protection

- Analysis of customer dependency (including, at minimum, largest customer sizes for past few years, as a percentage of total business)

- Major customer history (including, for any customer currently providing more than 5% of total sales, sales volumes at least three years back, by customer, and if possible projections forward for three years)
- Description of major customer contracts
- Analysis of total market size (broken down by major segments, if applicable)

In preparing information for buyers, it is critical to prepare thorough and well-documented information likely to be perceived as proven "truth" by the buyers. Sellers who focus all of their information upon unsubstantiated forward estimates for the future are often not regarded as credible. Eventually, as the selling process winds out, the seller will need to make a selection of buyers from offers he will obtain. If he has not provided information that will stand up to later scrutiny, the offers he receives initially **will** deteriorate in later stages of investigation as buyers become uncertain or insecure about information reliability.

A recent article in M & A News *estimated that more than sixty percent of early letters of intent failed to close last year. This is a frightening statistic—especially considering the fact that it doesn't even address those deals which did close, but did so at reduced pricing from the original proposal.*

Only by making sure that all of the early stage info is thorough and accurate, can you ensure high likelihood of closure, at the original terms proposed by the buyer.

In spite of this advice to provide thorough and detailed information to buyers, there may be times when due to potential competitive considerations, some information may need to be veiled to protect the seller. For example, we often label top customers as A, B, C, etc., and disclose the type of customer (nature of the customers business), but not names. This masking of customer names may be impossible for the extremely large major customer (like those with 30% or 40%-plus of total sales). However, for important but not critical individual customers, with, for example, perhaps 5% to 20% of total sales volumes, it is generally acceptable to buyers to have such trend information on a no-name basis.

Identifying & Investigating Buyers

THE VAST MAJORITY of business owners think they may well know who the "best" buyers are likely to be for their companies. After twenty years of operating in this business, we have learned that ninety percent of the time, they are wrong. (By the way, we also don't always know who the best buyers may be—until much later, after exhaustive investigation).

The obvious direct competitor is often the first buyer considered. While it may be absolutely true that you, as a competitor, are a thorn in their side, and that they would love to have you removed from the competition, that is rarely a great reason for them to pay a premium price. I can't tell you how many sellers have said to me " ABC Company would pay X million dollars, just to get rid of us!" Experience has taught me that buyers VERY rarely (almost never) pay premium pricing "just to get rid of" a competitor.

The **best** buyers are usually companies slightly adjacent, but not too similar to yours. For example, a company, which sells much different products to the same type of customers as yours, might benefit enormously by adding your products to their mix. They can sell their other products to your customers, and thus increase volumes without harm of any product overlap to either your customer mix, or their own. They can also sell your products or services to their already established customers. One plus one becomes three! That's the ideal blend.

Or if a perspective buyer offers products or services like yours to a different customer category, the blend, again, can result in a multiplication impact. Customer base is widened, and facilities or operations that previously served only one type of customer base can now expand to more! Add that to a nice geographic diversity, which also enables service to a greater geographic range, for *both* companies, and the "win" can be enormous.

So... how do you find and identify these slightly "off-center" buyers who may create the premium fit? There are a number of wide-ranging potential sources for such buyers. Think creatively, out-of-the-box, about where adjacent players may be found. Ideally, you seek buyers who are financially healthy and are acquisitive, and who may be aggressively looking toward new directions to nurture growth. We have probed suppliers of raw materials to learn of new ideas or early stage growth strategies that suppliers are hearing about in the industry. We have explored capital equipment supply chains—talking to top sales people who may know who is expanding, and in what direction. We have even talked with major customers of our sellers (quietly and carefully, of course, without identifying who we're working for) to ask what an ideal supplier of goods or services might "look like" in their industry. (What would the range of products or services include to make them of optimal value to the customer? What products or services does the customer often find lacking or weak from existing suppliers?)

It can also be enormously helpful to exhaustively research recent trends in merger and acquisition activities in a segment.

> *Our firm has done an enormous range of business for material handling companies, including conveyor manufacturers, palla-tizers, bulk material movement systems, and others. Some years ago we realized that almost all of these material movement sup-pliers needed ever-increasing expertise in, and access to, high-end systems integration capabilities, and robotics. Every material handling function in the world is becoming increas-ingly dependent upon complex computerized functions to allow greater automatic sorting, routing, trucking, and labeling of goods being moved. As a result the "systems integrators" became*

almost the pivotal element of the system to be sold. Those became great powerhouse sellers! The biggest and best also became great influence brokers regarding hundreds of other material handling systems components. The manufacturers of the other product categories found that they could increase power with their customers enormously, if they also owned strong systems integration capabilities.

As industries evolve and change (like this example in material handling), it pays to take notice of changes and to talk to leading industry experts about the evolving trends, and what it may mean to merger and acquisition activities. We talk to officers and trade association leaders within industry groups (both direct industry or trade groups, which fit with our clients, and "adjacent" trade groups likely to be influenced by common trends). We interview dozens of trade publication editors and reporters about trends and changes looking into the future.

We also interview dozens of sellers from recent years, from companies similar to our clients. Ideally we would like to know who approached them, and why, and who was highly aggressive in bidding for their acquisition. We learn all we can about how buyers determine pricing, and what models they use to ascertain value. Past sellers of private companies can be hard to find—and of course not all will talk. However, if they know that the information that they pass along will be respected as private, and held very closely, and if they know that it is asked in service to another seller (in the same shoes that they were once in) many *will* share very helpful information.

First Approaches to Buyers

THE FIRST APPROACHES we make to buyers who we have prescreened and determined to be viable targets for our client-seller, are made with the request that a nondisclosure agreement be signed before we name or identify our client-seller. We utilize a seller ID number in the confidentiality agreement initially, and then proceed AFTER signing to identify our seller client.

This is, naturally, almost impossible for the seller to do without independent help. However, in virtually every case, it remains strongly advisable to get a written understanding of the agreement to secrecy in place at the very outset of discussions. Buyers understand and expect to make such a commitment and it should not cause any hardship to the relationship to ask for the commitment.

Normally as we make these early approaches, we already have a fairly strong knowledge of what is likely to be of interest to the buyer. Immediately after they sign the non-disclosure, we then provide them with a brief (two to three page) narrative overview about the company, and a one page financial summary of sales, margins, profitability levels, and key asset information. If we have done a good job in selecting the companies to approach in this manner, nine out of ten of those we contact will come back to us quickly, within days or even hours, to ask for more information. If it's a great fit, it tends to be apparent almost immediately, and the prudent buyer is ready to move very quickly.

We also find these early-stage discussions with buyers to be an important learning step to understand what key items those buyers are most eager to know for the next phase assessment. Although we do at this stage have a full core set of information ready to exchange with buyers, there often will be specific inquiries, which may cause us to enhance or expand exhibits to cover areas of special interest to particular buyers.

> *Several years ago we were in the process of selling a general contracting construction firm, which had some most impressive large contracts in process. Buyers quickly requested detailed information on our past history of large contract profitability, and began very early on to estimate "value" of our pending contracts. In this instance we were able to demonstrate with absolute*

certainty that every project the company had completed for the past ten years had resulted in pretax profits at the level of 25% or more, of total sales. Our client's backlog in this instance was about $65 million in sales (this on a company at only a bit under $30 million in sales at the time), so we began presenting a "FMV of assets and contracts pending" exhibit, which gave wonderful support to a value far above what a simple multiple of earnings might have shown. The company sold at a very handsome premium, with three offers in the end above $50 million for stock of the selling company.

Early inquiries by buyers helped us to know what information to develop and demonstrate for this seller.

Letter of Interest

WHEN BUYERS HAVE received strong and thorough fundamental information about the prospective seller, and they continue to have a strong interest, they will next often request a visit to the seller's business location, to be accompanied by a face-to-face meeting with owners. The difficulty in granting such early requests to all buyers who make these inquiries lies in the potential for this to require actually dozens of full-day meetings with potential buyers. Also, many of the buyers who inquire may have little substantial interest in the purchase. They are curious, they are learning about the marketplace and what sellers may be out there and available, but they may not have any viable interest at a price-point likely to be of interest to the buyer.

Additionally, with each additional visit granted, there are several noteworthy and significant disadvantages to sellers:

(1) Substantial time is utilized to muster appropriate people, and make them available for a half-day or longer. (This is a significant distraction from the basic tasks of running the business and keeping it healthy and trending well.)

(2) Multiple visitors increase the likelihood of employees discerning (and fearing) possibility of sale.

(3) Owners quickly become exhausted by these activities— reducing energy and velocity available for future (and perhaps better) buyers.

In order to keep the volume of intrusive visitors to a manageable and modest level, we normally request a non-binding "letter of interest" from buyers before even considering allowance of a personal visit to our seller-client.

The letter of interest is a non-binding expression of interest, which stipulates the expected price to be paid and any key terms which the buyer may require. For example, if the buyer will require the seller to accept any non-cash proceeds, such as a note to be paid over time, then the amount of the note, the interest rate, the timing, and collateral for the note must be outlined in the letter of interest. If the buyer will require the seller to retain ownership of some minority equity, that too must be specified and detailed. Any expected requirements for employment agreements must be specified.

Normally we will obtain at least eight to ten letters of interest from prospective buyers, and we will choose our client's favorite two or three buyers to invite for a visit. Also, these ten or so from whom we obtain a letter of interest are, if possible, the "best" buyers who are likely to pay the premium.

When such a letter is requested, buyers know that we will utilize the information they provide as a screening mechanism to determine whom to invite for a visit. This puts some pressure on the buyer to make a proposal that has a reasonable chance to be desirable and of interest to the seller. We have found from many years of experience that most buyers are realistic and reasonably firm with the initial forays they put forward in the letters of interest. We have virtually never had a buyer return to our seller with a lesser monetary proposal between this stage of the engagement and the letter of intent. We have had buyers who, after the visit, decided they did not wish to continue the pursuit, but this has not been for pricing issues. It has been for other issues that caused the buyer to become uncomfortable with the level of risk in the venture.

Several years ago we sold a packaging company in California that serviced premium computer companies around the world, including such giants as HP, Microsoft, Epson, and others. These were extremely difficult-to-serve clients—very demanding and very stringent about expectations in pricing, in quality, and in virtually every aspect of service. We requested letters of interest for our client seller from twelve of our best suitors, and we chose the top three offers from those letters to invite for tours of the facility and meetings with owners. During the first visit we conducted, the buyer sat down with the CEO/ Seller at the end of the tour, and asked his most important question. He said, "You have done a tremendous job at maintaining strong margins and solid repeat volumes with some of the most difficult-to-please customers in all of our industry. Tell me ... how have you achieved this so remarkably, in this extremely tough and competitive industry?" Our client sat back in his chair, folded his arms, and tapped his temple with his index finger, while telling the buyer, "It's all right here!"

That buyer was gone, within the hour, never to return. No buyer wants to buy a company that is entirely dependent upon one owner. The sad part is that, of course, it wasn't true. That company had great people at many levels within, and had developed a phenomenal set of team mechanisms to KEEP those power-house customers always happy, and ever-reaching for more of the company's great services and great products. We sold the company well, and it continued quite successfully, but the very first "letter of interest" melted to nothing, all too quickly.

The timing for obtaining such early stage letters of interest would ideally be at one moment, for all buyers simultaneously. That is not always achievable, but it's a sensible and worthy target. If other buyers progress later to the point where they know what they might offer, while requesting next steps such as the visit, they can then be asked for a letter of interest before owners decide how to proceed. If their proposals are aggressive and exciting, it's always okay to later add one more suitor to the process, as long as no exclusive dealings commitment has been signed.

Site Visits by Buyers

ALMOST EVERY BUYER who sees information about the company and who may have an interest in it will try to arrange a site visit. Normally, only a handful of such visits should be allowed.

When buyers visit, they normally tour the facility like any outside guest (such as customers, insurance companies, and bankers) and employees will not be told that they are prospective buyers.

In advance of such visits a general clean-up of facilities is advisable. Operations should appear clean, well organized, and safe for workers. As buyers tour a plant, it is important to require normal safety gear at any manufacturing facility (hard hats, safety glasses, etc.). For manufacturers the attention should be focused in advance of the visit on cleanliness of space, on clear separation and/ or demarcation of hazardous or waste materials, and on removal or cleanup of any old inventories of raw materials or finished goods. For office locations cleanliness is also important, but so too is a reasonably calm and positive appearance of staff. You may need to alert the staff that visitors are coming, and that you would appreciate a positive and professional appearance.

Every company has its own history and norms for expectations with respect to touring guests, and you, as knowledgeable owners, will need to coach your intermediary on what might work best. I have had clients describe us as bankers, as prospective insurance representatives, as old friends or relatives, and any number of other things.

Generally, any of these descriptions can work well, but do keep in mind that you are likely to have several such visits within a fairly short time frame, so it's best not to make excuses that seem to be unique and one time events. (That could require difficult and less plausible excuse-making, particularly if you might end up arranging as many as four or five visits before you complete the process.) Also, visiting buyers will need to be told how to identify themselves upon arrival, and who to ask for or speak with.

Sometimes tours for the buyer can alternatively be done at night or during week ends, when no staff members are there to become curious. This is fine, but buyers generally would much rather s ee your operation in action, if this is possible. It's amazing how much the buyer can glean, just by observing how employees greet you and how they react to your observation.

> *We once sold an old-line steel manufacturer, where the owner consistently donned suit coat and tie to show people around the plant. I think there were only two people in the plant in total who I ever saw the owner speak to. As we walked through the plant, workers averted their eyes, did not speak at all, and generally seemed intimidated. Every buyer wanted to see the plant in action, but those who toured inevitably came away with less eagerness.*

The sellers' intermediary should make clear in advance of the visit that wandering around the facility alone at any time is not permitted, and that casual inquiries or conversations with staff are also not allowed. The intermediary should coordinate identification processes and arrival time for guests, the kind of dress preferred by sellers, and any other logistical details important to maintenance of confidentiality.

In preparing for these visits, we normally try to design a set of "sample" questions that we think the buyer is likely to ask. This is a healthy pre-visit exercise, and can make you, as seller, much more comfortable because you will have thought through in advance how you might respond to the most likely questions.

Buyers will ask about anything they see that looks unusual in the operation. They will ask about old inventory or supply items that look infrequently used. They will ask about disposal of waste or man-ufacturing byproducts. They will ask about the owner's reason for considering sale. They will ask about strengths and weaknesses. They will ask about sales and marketing prognosis for the future. They will ask about possible big-picture changes to come for the industry.

After the visit, arrangements should be made for buyers and seller to meet off-site at some confidential location to invite questions and become better acquainted. If there are key management staff members who are privy to the selling process, such staff members may also be invited (although in most cases this would not be required by buyers).

Also, during the post-visit discussion time there is generally time and opportunity for the seller to ask questions of the prospective buyer. Sellers may seek histories and results of prior acquisitions this buyer has made. Sellers may inquire about what governance mecha-nisms are expected by the buyer, and key staffing additions or changes the buyer thinks will occur. Sellers may want to know how much debt the buyer would expect the entity to bear. They may have interest in the buyer's desire for additional subsequent add-on acquisitions to further grow this segment of the business.

All of these things, and more, come together to help the sellers to arrive at conclusions about which buyers they really hope to con-summate a deal with.

If a seller conducts two to three visits of this type, such as on-site tours for prime buyers, the seller will often know immediately after each visit which buyer is preferable to work with. If that buyer was likewise favorably impressed, he or she will often intend to submit a letter of intent within days following such a visit. The race for the finish has begun!

Letter of Intent/Outline of Terms

WHEN BUYERS HAVE looked at well-documented early information on a company they perceive as a strong fit, they are often amazingly quick to come forward with a proposed letter of intent. The normal letter of intent will state a purchase price and will then ask for the seller to sign acceptance of an "exclusivity commitment," whereby they agree not to continue discussions with other buyers.

There is very little advantage to the seller for accepting such a proposal. Usually the seller gets nothing for such acquiescence, while the buyer neatly and effectively removes all competition from the acquisition process.

After the letter of intent is in hand, the buyer then goes on to spend significant time and money in study of the acquisition. This is normally the buyer's stated reason for requiring the seller's agreement to a letter of intent. It is absolutely true that this process is costly and time consuming for the buyer. It is also costly and time consuming for the seller. Both buyer and seller will have significant staff time, CPA costs, and legal fees from this point forward.

Recent estimates say that something between fifty and seventy-five percent of deals that have signed letters of intent never get to closing. Additionally, of the deals that do get to closing, probably half of those deals do so only after reduction of purchase price because of problems discerned by buyers in due diligence.

Our firm normally resists acceptance of any letter of intent, unless or until we can obtain a non-refundable deposit from the buyer first. (The deposit is not truly non-refundable, but it is non-refundable for a discretionary change of heart by the buyer.) The seller will have to refund the deposit, in almost every case, if the information provided has been materially incorrect in any way. Also, in some cases, there may be no buyer willing to make the non-refundable deposit. If we can't obtain a deposit, we would prefer to then go directly to close, with no "letter of intent" stage in between. That way the buyer still has the pressure of knowing that if they become unreasonable about terms, or if they attempt to change price, we still have other buyers alive and well.

In about one third of our transactions we do get a nonrefundable deposit. In another one third, we go directly to closing, with no letter of intent. Alas, for the last one third, we may end up having to accept a letter of intent before closing.

In our firm's first fifteen years of operation we had only *one* deal with a signed letter of intent that did not close. In the past several years, however, we have had about one deal per year which reached letter of intent stage, but then later failed. Fortunately, all except one of those deals did subsequently close with other buyers. However, it's costly and exhausting to have to start over.

Part of this shift and the increased difficulty in today's market is due to the much stronger presence of equity fund buyers. Almost all of the failed deals we have experienced to date have been with equity fund buyers. Equity funds are so very eager to drive away competition that they are quick to sign letters of intent—and then will later decide if it's really worth buying.

There are several key mechanisms to help a letter of intent have a better chance of completion. First and most importantly, it is very helpful to detail key elements of the deal in the letter of intent. For example, it should include:

> • Purchase price payment terms (cash, or, if notes, the timing, interest, collateral, guarantees for payment, restrictions for management fees, and restrictions regarding owner takeout of dividends or significant assets)

> • General content of representations and warranties, and related caps on indemnifications

> • Timing for due diligence, financing firm-ups, definitive agreement draft, rent agreements, employment agreements, or other ancillary agreements, and a "drop dead" closing date

- Access during due diligence (specify employee interviews allowed, and if due diligence will be conducted off-site or on)

Additionally, if you can't come to agreement with a buyer regarding either a deposit or a very narrow time frame on the letter of intent, get creative:

- Instead of deposits, consider a financial penalty to be paid by the buyer to cover seller costs if the buyer drops out for discretionary reasons.

- If you can't agree on issues of employee access, consider granting such access before closing, but only very late in the game (perhaps in the last week before close). That way the buyers will have significant investment before they risk your employee relationships and, if they decide not to close, you will have the ability to say very quickly "The deal is off. Don't worry, employees." (Less time means reduced risk to the seller.)

- If the buyer worries that the deposit might be at risk because you, the seller, might be unreasonable about terms for the final definitive agreement, offer to negotiate and sign the definitive ahead of closing, with the deposit to be made, and with the exclusivity to be granted, only at signing. (Most buyers can produce the first draft of a definitive purchase agreement within a week or two. With focus from advisors and attorneys on both sides, the issues can be negotiated and resolved within another week or two. In the meantime, the other big worries for the buyer can likely clear the due diligence process. A phase one environmental review, for example, can be scheduled and completed within a few weeks. Accounting due diligence usually takes no more than perhaps two weeks—although scheduling of the buyers' CPAs for the time required often adds another week or two. Nonetheless, a sense of urgency on timing can usually result in completion of most of the due diligence efforts in less than a month in total time.)

• Sellers often prefer, if possible, to keep secrecy about the possible pending transaction until closing. Buyers want access for their CPAs, environmental consultants, and sometimes others for as long as possible in advance of closing. Almost all buyers can commit to a sixty-day time frame for due diligence. Access can be granted only on a confidential basis, done under the guise of new financing lenders or shareholder evaluations for estate planning. Alternatively, existing sellers' CPAs can be brought into the process and can obtain almost everything, for which the buyers' advisors will need to verify records.

A letter of intent that the seller does sign should include a clear provision that the exclusivity commitment is voided immediately if the buyer proposes a material change in price or terms. This is a critical and important protection to the seller, and it causes the buyer to consider items carefully and to propose such changes in terms only when or if they are truly ready to walk away from the transaction.

Letters of intent should also be specific with details of any ancillary agreement which will be required as part of the deal. Employment agreement terms should be outlined as well as noncompete timing and general descriptions of noncompete coverage.

If the seller owns real property in a separate entity, which will then continue to be leased to the buyer, the rental rates and related timing or duration of the commitment needs to be specified. Additionally, any desired option to buy such property from the seller needs to be explicitly detailed. (Buyers will often want a first right of refusal if sellers later decide to sell the property. This is fine and can work satisfactorily for both parties, but sellers need to ensure that the terms of such agreements give them adequate freedom to market the property openly in this event.)

If the buyer requires employment agreements from any key staff beyond the owner group, this too must be negotiated early with the letter of intent. If the buyer does not want to consummate the purchase without such employee agreements signed in advance by certain people, then the seller's risk to his employee relationships will go up dramatically as the buyer attempts negotiations with his staff. If the buyer is simply assuming continuation of already existing employment terms, such risk is much reduced, and far more likely to be palatable for both seller and for existing staff.

ESOP as the Buyer

BUSINESS OWNERS COMMONLY hear of the use of an "ESOP" in planning for a management buyout. It is presented as a wondrous and magical vehicle by some, and as a dangerous nightmare by others. Like most business tools it is not magical or deadly—it simply needs to be used in appropriate circumstances.

An ESOP is an Employee Stock Ownership Plan. It is a special type of tax-qualified Profit Sharing Plan, which invests in company stock, instead of in marketable securities.

Basically, the prime advantages are as follows:

(1) If the owner sells stock to the ESOP, and realizes a gain on the sale, income tax on such gain may be deferred, as long as the owner invests the proceeds of the sale in domestic equity securities (i.e., a U.S. stock).

(2) If the ESOP borrows money to finance a portion of its stock purchase, the company may then make tax-deductible contributions to the ESOP to enable it to service the debt—both interest and principal.

(3) If the ESOP borrows money, it may be able to do so at below market rates, because of certain tax advantages the bank can gain on interest income from the ESOP.

(4) The trustees of the ESOP vote the shares, which it owns. Such trustees may be officers of the company and/or key management members. Thus an owner who is still active in the company can retain management control, as long as he is willing to operate the company fairly and rationally, in the best interests of all beneficial shareholders.

(5) If a company is 100% ESOP-owned, and that company elects Subchapter S tax status, the ESOP-owned shares are not taxed on annual income. Although it is not certain that this benefit will remain long term, as long as it does prevail, this can be an extraordinary advantage in providing improved cash flow for the company to service debt.

Given these tremendous advantages, the ESOP sounds like (and can be) a tremendous tool for tax-advantaged sale. However, it won't always work. In order to determine if it's a likely fit, owners need to consider the following:

(1) *Is there an employee group with significant retirement money already tucked away?* In many cases, employees may have participated for years in other types of employer sponsored retirement plans. If they have, and savings accumulated are substantial in such plans, employees may be able to convert their accumulated retirement funds to equity in the ESOP investment. This may provide the capital that the employee group needs to make the transaction viable.

(2) *Is there a strong upper-to-middle management group, that will have the ability to run the company effectively?* Chances are, the ESOP will have to finance a portion of its purchase. If the owner intends to exit, the ESOP will not be able to obtain such financing unless a bank or other investor can be convinced that the successor management group will run the Company well.

(3) *Are there at least a handful of key members of management who will be the prime leaders (and/or major beneficial owners) of the buyout, and are such key management* *players willing to personally guarantee debt?* Generally, if the owner is selling all or a large majority of his stock to the ESOP, the ESOP is likely to need to borrow to pay the exiting owner. In such case the lender will likely want personal guarantees from key management members, both in connection with new amounts to be loaned, and possibly in connection with a request to remove the exiting shareholder from personal debt guarantees already in place. Management members will only be motivated to take on this responsibility if they are confident of their capabilities, and excited about the prospect of significant ownership. The bank may prefer to defer removal of the former owner from debt guarantees until it watches the success of the new management team for a time, but this is less likely if several other key people step up to replacement of those guarantees. (Even with far less substantial assets behind the guarantees of a management team, their raw willingness to "bet" on themselves significantly improves the odds for enthusiastic bank support.)

(4) *Is payroll large enough to allow adequate contributions to the ESOP in future years to service the debt?* If the ESOP has to borrow, as an example, $1,000,000 to complete a stock purchase, it will have debt service obligations of principal and interest, over a period that may range, typically, from five to ten years (ten year amortization is fairly common, with an earlier balloon date). For purposes of this example, let's assume the ESOP payment required would be $150,000 per year. Generally, ESOP contributions are limited to 15% of payroll. Thus, in this example, annual payroll would have to be around $1,000,000 per year, in order to allow a base for a $150,000 annual tax-deductible contribution to the ESOP. If the company's aggregate annual payroll costs were only $300,000 per year, the maximum tax-deductible contribution would be around $45,000—not enough to service the ESOP debt planned.

Although it still might be possible to use the ESOP advantageously for a part of the stock purchase, the $1,000,000 originally contemplated to be borrowed would not be feasible.

(5) *Are there outside investors who would like to purchase the company, and who have substantial retirement moneys of their own from other corporate retirement plans?* Sometimes individual buyers come to us who may have $500,000 or more form 401(k) or other corporate retirement plans from their previous employment. Under certain conditions, these moneys can be transferred to our client's company plan, and eligible for use to purchase stock through the newly formed ESOP. Such funds, combined with other personal funds of the buyer, and with other ESOP funds from employees, may help to make an otherwise difficult ESOP transition viable.

(6) *As exiting owner, do you anticipate a large taxable gain on sale of your company?* Most of the core benefits of an ESOP, from the exiting owner's viewpoint, relate to the tax deferrals available. If the gain would be substantial, and the tax significant, and if the owner can afford to leave the proceeds invested for some time post sale, (growing tax-deferred) the owner may be able to sell to the ESOP for well less than true cash value which an outsider would pay, and still retain the same or more "take-home" cash.

(7) *How strong is the alternative of sale to outsiders?* If the company is in an industry that is strongly aggressive in the acquisition market place, it may bring a disproportionately high price in sale. If strong commercial and industrial buyers will want your particular business for market share or for some special type of capability, they may compete ruthlessly in pricing their bids for purchase of the company in order to be sure they beat the competition. When this is the case, the competitive price point for purchase of the company can well be driven above any level that the employee group will ever reasonably be able to compete with, and successfully pay.

The best fit for the ESOP transaction (instead of independent sale) is commonly in the weaker market, where capitalized earnings and/or asset base would tell you that the company is worth more than what open market buyers are willing to pay. Examples? Construction or contracting companies in an economic slump. Old-line manufacturers with no growth potential, but fairly stable or very slowly dwindling sales levels. Companies with high asset book values, little debt, but disproportionately small recurring earnings levels (borrowing base good, earnings enough that liquidation doesn't make sense, but not much competitive market for purchase).

If you think ESOP purchase may be fit for your company, where do you go from here? In general, the first step in considering an ESOP is to walk through the individual circumstances to assess the financial viability of an ESOP buyout. An experienced consultant can tell you what percentage employee participation to expect, how much bank financing is realistic, and what sort of operating cash flow the company would need to make it successful.

On the flip side, what are some of the pitfalls?

(1) ESOPs seem to work especially well when they can fund enough cash to do all or nearly all of the purchase in one swoop. When only a portion of the stock can be purchased, or when the owner must remain on the hook for significant debt, the risk increases dramatically. If operations fail, the owner may have to return to run the company, and his option for sale to outsiders is significantly impaired. The company has done poorly at this stage, which is why the owner has returned with a problem. Outside buyers do not hasten to take a minority interest. Nor are they eager to "marry" a failing management group, which owns stock in the company through an ESOP.

(2) In reviewing ESOP potential, owners need to be particularly careful to assess viability before talking to management employees. It is very difficult to invite employees to consider ownership, and then to withdraw the invitation, in favor of sale to outsiders. Employees become disgruntled, and outside buyers may be fearful of employee retention issues.

(3) When stock is owned by an ESOP, the stock is voted by its Trustees. Such trustees must act in the best interests of the shareholders as a whole. This means that the trustee has a fiduciary responsibility not to take wild and excessive benefits or salary withdrawals personally (the three week trips to attend half-day seminars in Europe are probably out).

(4) Companies, which are partially owned by an ESOP, may be less desirable to buyers. Don't expect to sell part of your stock to an ESOP today, and then sell the rest to an outside buyer tomorrow. The ESOP shareholders can be made to sell at a later date, by the trustees, but buyers generally are loathe to come in as the "bad guys" who forced the employees to give up stock ownership. Also, trustees may face fiduciary liability if there could be any doubt whatsoever as to the adequacy of the price attained.

(5) ESOPs are costly to implement and costly to administer. They require formal initial and periodic valuations of the company by an independent source, and careful adherence to a complex set of federal rules and regulations. It is foolish and dangerous to enter into these transactions without specialized legal advice—in spite of the fact that such advice is costly. Count on spending at least $25,000 to $75,000 to get the plan started and the purchase in place. Additionally, you will be required to have an annual audit of the plan, probably at least a CPA's review of the company, a valuation of the company, and a far more modest, but still important level of ongoing legal advice as ESOP rules change and plan participants come and go over the years.

In summary, when are ESOPs usually most effective? When:

(1) The owner will have substantial gain on sale, and thus a significant benefit from the tax deferral

(2) The employee salary base is sizeable, allowing hefty contributions to fund debt repayment by the ESOP

(3) There is a strong middle management group—preferably with four to six financially stable and professionally capable people—eager to become owners and willing to guarantee debt

(4) There is a predecessor retirement plan which has been in place for a time, which may allow capital transfer for ESOP stock purchase

(5) The external markets for possible purchase of the company are not particularly strong or aggressive

The company needn't score a "10" on all of the above for the ESOP purchase to be a fit. If very few of the above five criterion are met, however, it's unlikely to work. If, on the other hand, most do seem to be reasonably well met, chances are quite good that an ESOP is a viable and productive option, which should be at least examined as one possible exit strategy.

Some years ago we assisted a management group in buyout of the former owner, via an ESOP. In order to achieve financing for the transaction, four of the top management employees had to personally guarantee significant debt. They did so, and they went on to do a tremendous job in running the company—paying down significant debt very aggressively in the next several years. The company was entirely ESOP-owned, so the avoidance of corporate income tax, via a Subchapter Selection, contributed well to cash flow, allowing even more rapid repayment of debt.

The company was originally purchased at an overall valuation level of approximately $15 million. We later sold the com-

pany, in an aggressive and highly competitive process, to out-siders, about five years after the purchase. We sold the company for $80 million—all cash! A dedicated and very hard-working employee group profited immensely! This was the classic happy ending to a wonderful ESOP buyout!

Due Diligence

AS THE BUYER progresses toward completion of the transaction, he will necessarily need to verify that the information he has been given about the company is accurate, and that he has a good grasp on risks to the company's business. If the seller has done a thorough job of documenting and disclosing such information, this should not be a particularly dangerous or difficult process.

We will divide this discussion into several major segments, which most transactions involve.

Financial Due Diligence

Buyers will commonly hire their independent CPAs to verify accuracy of financial information they have been given. If the seller has audited financial statements from his own independent CPA (or even reviewed financial statements), much of this process can be conducted at the offices of the seller's CPA firm, by review of the detailed working papers maintained by that CPA, and interviews with the partner or other lead people involved on the engagement. Buyers will also probably wish to review internal financial statements for the latest interim period to date, and will want to compare such monthly financials to those from the same period last year to scan for significant changes in the business performance during the year in process. They may also wish to verify information they have received on top customer histories, on gross margin histories by product line, or on significant cost issues they have inquired about (such as perhaps research and development, unusual non-recurring costs from recent operations, histories of capital expenditures, etc.) Normally this exercise in its entirety is not terribly time-consuming (typically no more than a few weeks, tops), but naturally this will depend in part on the quality of external CPA validation available, and on the quality of internal financial information available on a regular monthly basis.

Environmental and Regulatory Matters

Buyers will ask to see histories of any environmental reviews or histories, particularly for manufacturing operations. Today almost every real estate purchase will require a Phase I Environmental review, so if the building was purchased within the past fifteen years or so, it almost certainly had a Phase I review at that time. If real estate is to be a part of the purchase, such reviews will almost certainly need to be updated. Additionally, if the company deals with emissions regulations or if there have been OSHA reviews or issues, all histories of any such regulatory status will need to be carefully reviewed and considered by buyers. These reviews are commonly required by all buyers, but they also will probably be required by lenders to consummate any commitments for loaned proceeds to finance the transaction.

Marketing Due Diligence

Buyers will investigate market size information they have been given, and will commonly add to that with their own investigations of market size, trend information and prognosis data, and information on recent or pending changes in the industry. Buyers also commonly seek whatever data they can get to assess solidity of customer relationships and prognosis for future growth and continued volumes. If any one single customer provides as much as perhaps 30% to 40% of the volume or more, it is almost certain that the buyer will seek to have some level of contact with the big customer, to ensure their likelihood of continuance. Sellers are naturally concerned about such contact, and rightly so. It may be possible to meet the buyer's need for assurance here by conducting customer satisfaction surveys by phone, and allowing the buyer to listen in. Alternatively, near the end of the due diligence time, it may be possible to introduce the buyer as a new employee, and allow the two to become better acquainted that way.

> *Some years ago we sold a company with a major customer concentration in snowmobile parts for Polaris. As we approached the closing date, the company had a major annual event with Polaris staff, where our client's top sales people normally attended a two day planning meeting with Polaris executives, and spent some time each year in snowy Canadian forests, trying out the latest and greatest new product with Polaris staff. The lead person among our buyer group wanted to attend, and we were able to arrange it—introducing him as a new marketing resource for the company. The buyer came back with a report that the visit had gone wonderfully—except for the 40-below-zero degree outing at midnight for "fun" with the customer. The deal closed, and all ended happily, but I think the buyer remained fairly reserved about the "fun" midnight event.*

Management and Personnel Evaluation

Sometimes buyers will wish to talk to key employees, to assess their capabilities, or, perhaps more importantly (and more dangerously), to assess their likelihood of staying on staff after an ownership transition. This is something which should have been talked through and agreed upon with the first full outline of the purchase agreement, and is something which many sellers find extremely dangerous and intimidating. As a seller, you do not want your "deal" to be dependent upon whether or not the buyer and your staff like one another, or can craft an ongoing employment deal that both will sign off on. Most buyers will not insist upon employee interviews and discussions, except or unless there are a handful of very top-most employees that the company simply could not do without. Often if there is a COO or a top level manager who will be much needed for the company to continue well, he may have to be included in discussions before closing. Also, if there are key sales people, who could damage the company if they left to compete, they too may fit into this category.

If there are such key people with whom buyers may need contact, consider the following options:

(1) Sellers may want to include a "stay bonus" for key people, for the first few years of continued employment

(2) Sellers may delay interviews with such staff members until the last moment before close, to ensure that all else has passed in the due diligence process, and this is the last "risk" piece for the seller to take on in this process.

(3) If equity fund buyers are the likely winners of the deal, they may propose some sort of options or stock bonus elements, which could make them much more attractive to staff.

We have seen a lot of creative and unusual mechanisms to get the assurance the buyer may need, and still reasonably protect the seller's interest. Understand the buyer's issues, be patient, and get creative, and you can almost always find some way to meet the needs of both sides.

Definitive Purchase Agreement

THE DEFINITIVE PURCHASE AGREEMENT (or more commonly just "the Definitive" for short, by those of us who know it and love it) is the binding and conclusive agreement to detailed terms for sale of the company. It is a forbidding, exhausting, long compilation of complex legal language, which you better have very carefully reviewed and understood by your team of brilliant professionals.

One of my clients commented recently on the Definitive Agreement as follows: "Following this transaction by reading this document, is like trying to follow a plot in a bowl of alphabet soup!" It is long, and it is hard, but it is critically important to KEEPING your proceeds post sale, so it's worth some intense effort.

Briefing readers on all of the intricacies of the issues pertinent here would be impractical, but I do want to alert you to just a few of the principal trouble spots most often misunderstood by sellers.

Structure and Terms

I am frequently amazed at the lack of clarity documents may provide about fundamental structure and terms. You, as a normal business person reviewing the document, should be able to clearly ascertain how much is being paid and what is being purchased. You should understand any mechanisms for post-closing adjustment, after a closing date audit is complete, and how any additional price paid or refund of price paid will be handled.

If there are deferred payments, such as notes to be paid over time by the buyer, consider carefully their collectability. I would always opt for cash over any deferred payment, even if it means quite a bit less in price. It is hard to protect against non-collection risk. If the cash up front isn't enough to induce you to sell, think twice (no—more than twice) before you count on deferred payments. If you must allow deferred payments, protect them aggressively. If the buyer is corporate, they are likely to form a shell acquisition corporation to do the deal. Make the parent company guarantee. If the buyer is an individual, require personal guarantees. Furthermore, if the spouse doesn't sign too, that personal guarantee may be virtually worthless when it's time to collect. Get a second deed of trust on a home. Get a deep pocketed relative's guarantee. Beef up every possible protection, or don't count on getting the deferred payments.

If there are payments contingent upon future performance, be very meticulous in how you define the performance bogies. Performance targets can be made impossible to achieve by a buyer imposing heavy intercompany or administrative charges, by changes in accounting methods, or by many other diversions of sales or profits. The simpler and more easily defined the targets are, the more possible it will be for you to avoid later dispute, and thus protect your rights.

My strong suggestion in all of the issues relative to fundamental pricing and terms is to make sure your CPA or other astute financial advisors also review this document. If there are discrepancies or confusing issues, insist on reworking them until all questions are clearly eliminated.

Representations, Warranties, and Indemnifications

Every seller will be asked to make representations and warranties about the company he is about to sell. He will be asked to make a legal representation that he has been honest and truthful. Easy. However, he will also be asked to make a legal representation that nothing has occurred under his reign which will impair the future assets or performance of the company. Furthermore, he will be asked to promise to indemnify the buyer if some foul surprise from the past later pops up. Not so easy.

Keep in mind that if the buyer does not ask you for a pretty aggressive set of representations and warranties, something is wrong. If the buyer is paying an aggressive price for the company, he naturally will want your promise that he is getting exactly what you told him he's getting. If he asks for nothing, you should be worried, because it probably means he's getting a bargain.

Most sellers are comfortable making representations and warranties about things they know about. Honesty and full disclosure should not be issues. Correct reporting of liabilities can be ascertained by CPAs. Taxes for the period of ownership can't be escaped from in any case, so if later tax audits surface problems for the period prior to closing, it's no more burden than the owner already had.

However, owners become very nervous about things that may have occurred on their watch, but which they may not know about. Your professional negotiators should limit all possible representations and warranties to "the best of seller's knowledge." There should be a ceiling on aggregate possible exposure to any seller indemnifications post sale. There should be a threshold to prohibit multiple small dollar claims, with some sort of diminimus rule. If there is a truly critical exposure point, both buyer and seller might consider insurance to provide protection. This is a complex set of issues, but one worth patience and tenacity to achieve a balanced and reasonable outcome. When all is said and done, risk to the seller should be managed and limited, and should be nominal to the aggregate outcome, or the seller shouldn't do the deal.

Ancillary Agreements

There will probably be multiple ancillary agreements, such as employment agreements, noncompetes, leases perhaps, and more. Although ancillary, these are not unimportant elements to the transaction.

Employment agreements generally are much more easily enforced against the employer than the employee. Nonetheless, they should be established under terms that are bona fide terms, terms that the seller really can live with prospectively. Sometimes buyers like to divert part of the purchase price to an employment contract, in order to make payments tax deductible. However, if the agreement calls for full time employment, even if the buyer says that real full-time work will actually not be necessary, the seller should ascertain that he is truly comfortable living with the exact written terms of the agreement before he signs.

Most sellers really are happier in the end with a relatively short term employment agreement, even if they think they will likely prefer to stay longer. Until you and the new buyer live together for a while, it is very difficult to predict how much you will like the new working environment.

We have had sellers who thought they wanted to work for many years, who decided within three months that they would be gone the next day if possible. On the other hand, we have had sellers who wanted to be gone tomorrow, who later found that they were, to their surprise, having more fun than ever before. (Sometimes having the parent corporation do all of the administration and worry about financing growth can make running a company a lot more fun.) In either case, the requirement to renegotiate, if a longer term relationship is desirable, tends to make both sides of the deal nicer to one another post sale. It also gives the seller the clear freedom to do other things if it's not working.

Noncompete agreements will always be required in connection with sale, and are reasonable and necessary. However, sellers should make sure that the agreement they sign is sensibly limited to areas of business their companies are in at the date of sale, and isn't allowed to spill over to whatever new venue their buyer may choose to get into in the future. A reasonable time period for a noncompete is generally two or three years. I've seen some as brief as one year (infrequently), and a few as long as five (also infrequently). The date of inception of the noncompete is also important. Most buyers will require that the noncompete continue in effect for at least some time after employment ends. Sellers should be cognizant of the issue, and watch the effective dates.

The Definitive is the guts of your final sale agreement, and is worth time and torment to understand and protect, in spite of the complexity and length (usually 100+ pages, including exhibits). We often read as many as ten or more versions of the Definitive from start to finish in the course of one deal, with changes to every single page. Negotiation of the final agreement takes hundreds of hours, and may be as much as a third of the total time spent in getting the sale done. This is where those great professionals you have on your team should shine, and you deserve and should expect at least a couple of very thorough sessions to explain and strategize about the issues.

Employment Agreement

OFTEN THERE ARE any number of ancillary agreements to a purchase transaction, which are left until the absolute last minute to discuss and negotiate. There is danger in such delay, in that the seller may have little time to work through problems, or even to think about them.

With respect to an employment agreement between the new buyers and the "cashed out" seller, we suggest attention to the following:

- Duration of Agreement
- Salary and details for any bonus elements
- Some definition of job role and title
- Location of primary work station (and, if important to employee, limitations to travel requirements)
- Definition of benefits (insurance, retirement contributions, car, etc.)
- Exit mechanism permitted from both employee and company perspective

Before accepting a letter of interest, we usually require at least an outline of post closing employment terms, before accepting. Such definition might be as simple as:

"Buyer and Seller agree to enter into a mutually agreeable employment contract, for a minimum of a one year period, with salary at $X. It is understood and agreed that employee's role shall include senior management responsibilities, that employee will continue to be based in (name city), and that benefits shall be comparable to those offered currently to senior management members. At or after the end of the initial one year period, either party shall have the right to terminate employment with thirty days notice."

One of the most difficult points to define in these agreements commonly relates to definition of a bonus arrangement. Bonuses to be paid based on future financial performance are much easier to define based on sales or even gross margin data for the newly sold company. However, many buyers will much prefer to define "performance" based on net pre-tax income. If there is a bonus to be paid based on pretax income, it is probably important to exclude certain elements from such calculations. For example, pre-tax income for bonus calculation purposes might exclude:

- Management or director fees taken by equity firms or other new ownership parties

- Depreciation expense on major new capital enhancements added post sale

- Income or losses on corporate acquisitions added post-close

- Income or expense due to changes in accounting policies

- Income or losses on non-arms' length transactions with new corporate affiliates

Some years ago we sold a company with a large "earn-out" for future performance. The earn-out formula targeted a set pre-tax income level, and the benefit to be paid the seller was very significant—at $15 million if aggregate targets were reached over a three-year period. Our client seller had an employment agreement to act as president for this three-year period. About one year into the post-close period, the buyer, having recognized some truly excellent talent in our client's top management group, began to offer exciting opportunities to many management employees at the company, if they would transfer to other subsidiary entities owned by the new parent corporation. This clearly weakened our client's certainty of achieving the aggregate three-year targets. Our client did not want to foil opportunities for excellent staff to move elsewhere, and yet the amount potentially to be lost, if targets were not met, was terribly important. Furthermore, luring employees away was clearly a hindrance to our client's most effective performance as president of the company.

Our client explained the circumstances to us, and we returned to the buyer to renegotiate appropriate actions in these circumstances. The buyer wanted the president to remain and to try to re-develop new management. They were unwilling to pay *the earn-out immediately, even though they understood our objections, because our client would then have no incentive to remain in their employ. We ended up compromising. The buyer agreed to guarantee our earn-out payment in full, at the end of the three year period, and the seller agreed, in exchange for this promise to allow staff to be moved at will by the new corporate owners during this time period. At the end of the three-year period all of the $15 million was paid, as agreed, and in the meantime, several of the top people in the excellent management group had moved on to roles for management of bigger and more exciting corporate divisions.*

Leaseback from Shareholders

OFTEN THE CLOSELY held business may lease its primary operating facilities from related party real estate partnerships or LLCs. When the time comes to contemplate sale, the buyer may hope to simply continue to lease the property from the former owners. Even for those corporations that own their own real estate, this is a fairly common and normal request from the would-be buyer. Some buyers simply do not consider themselves adept in real estate management issues, and much prefer to tackle business ownership without this additional complication.

In designing a lease agreement with a new buyer of the company, sellers need to be careful to reasonably protect their interest as a "to-be-independent" lessor. Buyers normally will hope to lease the properties at a rental rate roughly comparable to what the business paid before. As long as such rate was reasonably set at a fair market level, this is likely to be tolerable to the seller. However, there are several spots in such negotiations, which often become a bit more difficult.

(1) Buyers of the business may want to preserve the right to buy the real estate in the future, if things go well. They may request an "option" to buy, or a "first right of refusal," in the event that the former real estate owners wish to exit and sell the real estate. This is common, and may be quite workable, as long as the real estate owner retains the right to move fairly quickly, without undue delay by the corporate lessee. One common mechanism to protect the lessee from hardship, is to allow a fairly lengthy time period between notice of either party's desire to exit, and the actual date of potential transfer. Most lessees, if given at least six to twelve months to exit, would either find such exit livable (because they would have adequate time to secure alternative space), or they would make an early and definitive move to secure purchase for themselves.

(2) Sellers often have fairly lax terms in their leases regarding who would be required to make needed capital improvements, if repair issues arise. This issue may not be clearly defined, because in leasing to themselves both parties had matching objectives and incentives. Thus, when the same parties were at interest for both the company and the real estate holdings, any needed CapX would naturally be viewed for the overall best protection of all involved. When a new buyer comes into the picture, that buyer will commonly seek a much more tightly defined set of parameters around which capital improvements would fall to the cost of the lessor, versus the company. This should be discussed early on with buyers, and reasonable compromise solutions need to be agreed upon for such guidelines.

(3) Buyers who are to be new lessees tend to seek permission in the lease structure to sublease at will, to protect themselves in the event that they don't require all of the space maintained before the transaction. Sellers who will become lessors generally prefer to maintain control of the right to lease, and are loath to give up this freedom easily. If the lease agreement stipulates requirements for facilities, and protection against environmental abuse, and if the buyer/lessee has deep enough pockets to protect or to reimburse the lessor for any resultant damages, this usually can be worked out to both parties' satisfaction. If the lessee is a shell corporation, or is not very substantial financially, and if its parent or financial investor wishes to not guarantee the corporate commitments by a parent or deeper pocketed investor, then the seller/lessors need to be far more careful and controlling in their view of sublease rights.

(4) Buyers seek inevitably to ensure strong control over operating costs in future years, often by limiting lease cost increases to set agreed upon levels in future years. If property values increase dramatically during the lease tenancy, it may be necessary to inject a safety mechanism for review and comparison to outside third party appraisals of rental values, in longer-term future years.

These lease elements can be critical determinants of cash flow to a seller for some years subsequent to a sale transaction. Thus, they are worth significant time and trouble to work through in advance of finalizing the sale. The exposure here for the seller may not be enormous, as long as the lease proceeds are adequate to service any remaining debt on the property. However, even with debt covered, we generally would not recommend great risk for the property lessor beyond the first few years post sale.

Noncompete Agreement

ONE OF THE most sensitive "ancillary" agreements in any buy/sell arrangement often relates to the noncompete agreement which selling shareholders will be asked to sign in connection with the transaction.

Often buyers will propose terms to the noncompete that say the seller shall not be allowed to participate, as an employee or as a shareholder, in any venture which either the sold entity itself, or the purchasing entity, may be in competition with. The difficulty with this sort of wide-sweeping prohibition lies in the facts that: **(a)** the seller may not be aware of all areas of business touched by the buyer corporation, and **(b)** if the time period is defined to include some years forward from the transaction date, the purchasing corporation may later decide to expand its reach into any variety of new and more diverse holdings—thus putting new prohibitions in front of the exiting seller.

We generally push hard to try to limit the scope of noncompetes to businesses relating to the business being sold. This can significantly reduce the scope of businesses forbidden for the seller to become involved with in the future.

The time period of the noncompete also is critical. Most noncompete terms will run anywhere from two to five years post sale. Some will run throughout any period of actual employment by the seller (under ownership of the new buyer), and will extend anywhere from one to three years longer, post-employment. This is frankly a very reasonable and very normal protection that almost all buyers will seek to ensure time to establish their new team with customers, distributors, vendors, and others, after making a significant investment in their new venture.

If the seller has particular thoughts in mind about future potential endeavors, and is worried about their "allowability" in the mind of the buyer, we suggest they discuss the issue openly and directly, and try to "carve out" potential participation in areas of special interest to them.

> *Some years ago we dealt with a seller who had a consumer product company that was purchased by a far-reaching conglomerate, who sought protection against competition with any one of its subsidiaries. Our client was aware of several other companies who he found interesting as potential future investments he might some day become involved with. As we discussed terms of*

the noncompete, it became apparent that this could well become a source of conflict for our seller in the future.

The buyer was impressed by and enthusiastic about our seller's "eye" for future investments. We ended up carving out an arrangement whereby our seller agreed that if he were to invest in any one of several named areas, the buyer would be offered the right to participate in such investment with him, at a matching level. Our seller actually liked the arrangement, because it meant probable increased funding availability to him, if he chose to purchase one of those companies. It was a win/win for both sides, and the two continue to do transactions together today—some ten years later.

Post-Sale Payments & Protections

THERE ARE ANY variety of sensitive issues that may arise between buyers and sellers post sale, particularly if there are significant "back-end" proceeds to be collected.

One of the areas commonly discussed between buyer and seller is the intent of the buyers, regarding how long they intend to hold the investment, into the future. Sellers commonly prefer to know that the buyer they will enter into a deal with is not doing the transaction purely for the potential benefit of "flipping" the company—with sale to a new buyer, at a higher price, in the near future. Almost all buyers will assert at the outset that this is not their intent, and yet they prefer to maintain flexibility, just in case an exciting opportunity of this nature comes along. We have done many transactions where our sellers felt that this was an important issue, and where they worried about this possibility, because they felt that it COULD be the plan of the buyer—because either **(a)** the buyer might be willing to talk to long time adversaries, which the seller would not consider, or **(b)** there was potential for movement in their industry for much higher values in the future. We have found that in these cases it may well be acceptable to the buyer to insert a "claw-back" provision, which says if the entity is re-sold during the next few years for an increased price, the buyer agrees to share a portion of such a "win" with the exiting seller. Normally when this is done, the time period forward is not terribly lengthy (it may be just one to three years post sale), and often any resulting residual benefit to the seller will decline in future years, fairly rapidly. None-the-less, it can be an important and potentially a very valuable protection to the selling shareholders.

The most common, and probably the simplest item requiring protection post sale involves security the seller may be able to obtain with respect to any notes receivable taken as part of the selling proceeds. There are any number of security mechanisms to better protect such notes, but one of the simplest (and most effective) may be a guarantee by an able third party. This may be as simple as a personal guarantee from an individual buyer (and his wife, if you want to clearly enforce it), or a guarantee by an able and strong parent company for the corporate buyer.

> *Some years ago we sold a painting contractor to two individuals, and we accepted a note for a significant portion of the consideration. The buyers themselves were not wealthy, so their personal guarantees would not have been terribly meaningful by themselves. However, because the notes were an important part of the aggregate consideration, we would not accept just the personal guarantees of the parties, alone. We could have and would have turned to alternative buyers, unless the buyer could show further support for the guarantees. One of the individuals involved had a wealthy and successful father, who was willing to guarantee the note.*
>
> *A few years later the son of the guarantor wished to leave and re-sell his ownership interest to move on to other endeavors. We decided that we would not release the father from his guarantee, unless he either repaid the obligation in full, or secured asset*

pledges adequate to protect our seller's note. We ended with the obligation paid in full, but we would never have achieved that without the father's guarantee.

There are any number of other protections the seller may seek to protect a note. There are protections which allow for acceleration of the note in the event of certain events—like taking on of new outside debt, or if new acquisitions are to be made, or if the seller's employment is terminated before the payments are complete. Penalties often may be built into the debt if payments are late or if professional fees must be incurred by the seller to collect. Sellers may require that they have a board position until the note is repaid, or that at least they have the right to ongoing, timely financial information from the buyer. We have even seen transactions where default on any principal repayment voided the seller's noncompete, so the seller could, if desired, re-initiate business with old customers in a new company if he felt that he could recapture greater proceeds through that mechanism.

There are a wide array of creative and effective mechanisms to protect back end note proceeds, and it pays to consider such alternatives extensively. No note is ever as good as cash at close. If the seller MUST accept a note, he or she is well advised to secure it with every possible means.

A fair number of transactions today, especially in the smaller, closely held business venues, will encounter proposals for a portion of the proceeds to be paid on an "earn-out" basis, if certain operating targets are met during the years after sale. This can be a decent way to maintain some potential "upside" to the transaction, but it requires some fairly cautious negotiation to protect the seller. Earn-out formula benefits typically work much better, and have far less chance for later misunderstanding or litigation, if those formulas are tied to a targeted sales number, or even a targeted gross margin. Buyers tend to prefer to tie any such proceeds to their net income to reduce risk. If an earn-out is to be tied to net income, however, it becomes critically important to carefully define what is to be included in net income for purposes of such earn-out calculation. (See also discussion under "Employment Agreements" to highlight some of the areas you may wish to exclude from such calculations.) It also is advisable to stipulate the dispute handling mechanism in the event that the parties disagree at a future date about how the tally is to be made. Commonly a buyer's CPA will have to produce an analysis of the calculation, the seller's CPA should have the right to review all records to see that they agree, and, if they do not, both parties should be required to agree on a third party to be chosen to re-tally the earn-out amount due.

Noncompete disputes can be another area where post-sale dispute mechanisms can be helpful to ensure peaceful resolutions of any disagreements. Depending on the seller's future intentions, it may well be worthwhile to build into the agreement some means to peaceful solution. We have seen agreements where the buyer had a right to participate with the seller in new ventures that were close to the selling company's business. We have seen agreements where sellers agreed that if they were to "take" business from one of the seller's old customers to a new venture, they agreed to pay a set amount for such business, based on sales or margins from prior years' activities. If the seller intends to retire and play golf for the foreseeable future, this may not be an issue worth consideration. However, if new ventures are likely to be in the future of the exiting seller, it is worth the time to plan to avoid problems for those new ventures likely to be targeted in the future.

The last major element we commonly see as a "back-end" issue relates to retained royalties or license fees, if the seller holds future rights to income from such items. Normally if we design a post-close royalty or license fee, we will require some set minimum payment under such agreement, in order to keep it active. That way if the buyer simply ignores the potential development of future sales in the stipulated arena, the seller at least retains the right to seek other avenues to nurture such sales. We have also designed agreements where the buyer specifically agreed to $X promotional expense, to support the sales of such product. Additionally, we have had provisions where agreement was in place for a reduced "sub-license" fee for any later resulting off-shoots of the original product licensed. A strong intermediary, or a savvy intellectual property attorney can give you good support on how to protect the back-end for these types of arrangements.

Shareholder Buy/Sell Agreement

VIRTUALLY EVERY PRIVATE corporation which admits outside investors or management members to the owner group will want some sort of buy/sell agreement to provide for stock to be recaptured in the event of shareholder exit. Pricing for these agreements can get enormously complex, and is critical to design effectively in the buy/sell agreement.

Most of the discussion herein will relate to the common buy/sell agreements put into place upon sale of a majority interest to an out-sider—usually either an equity investment group, or sometimes a strategic corporate acquirer who likes the concept of leaving some small share in the hands of the seller.

The purchasing shareholder often is willing to commit to purchase any remaining stock held, at whatever time the selling shareholder ceases to be employed by the company. In some cases, they also may agree to such repurchase in a fixed time period—perhaps three to five years later than the initial transaction—even if the selling shareholder should decide to stay and work longer.

The most difficult portion of these agreements generally relates to the definition of how the selling price will be determined in event of exit. Formula pricing is simplest, and least subject to future dispute. A typical formula might provide for value to be set at a multiple of pre-tax earnings. Such value would often be set at a slightly conservative level (less than full value paid at close), but then such value would be adjusted (at least annually, and often even quarterly or more) to be reflective of current earnings levels. For example, if the company was sold for an overall value of 5.5 to 6 times EBITDA, the buy-back formula might provide for a value set at 5 times EBITDA. This would be the value for a debt-free company, so the tallied valuation would also have any interest-bearing debt subtracted from the total. If the transaction was triggered at some time when earnings were exceptionally low, there would probably also be some sort of protection of the selling shareholder, to stipulate that the overall pricing cannot be lowered below book value of the company's stock. Or, alternatively, in a case where losses were especially large (say, more than 5–10% of total sales), the agreement might provide that no repurchase at all can be required at such times.

Sometimes the buyer might request a formula to be based on an average earnings record over a several year time period. This can be reasonable and acceptable, but in such cases, the average should be "weighted" heavily toward the most recent year. (Buyers in the independent marketplace will almost always base pricing on either the most recent completed year, the most recent running twelve-month period, or, if progress is steady and budgets are reliable, on budgeted earnings levels for the year currently in process.)

The common buyout provision for the equity group or strategic majority shareholder, who wishes to protect against the need to finance large equity purchases in times of stress, will also normally build in provision to get the buy-back financed over time, if needed. They may provide for payment to the exiting shareholder over a period of perhaps two to five years following exit. In those agreements, the price would normally be fixed and determined at the date of exit, and the obligation would bear interest at reasonable market rates, but the cash might actually be payable over several years.

These are reasonable and sensible mechanisms to protect the new owner who may be buying such stock back, but sellers also need to seek protection.

Sellers should look for mechanisms to ensure buy-back in the event of dramatic changes to operations. For example, it is often possible to reserve the right for the minority shareholder to approve certain major transactions, or, if he does NOT approve, rights may be reserved to allow him to require stock buy-back. The types of events which might trigger such rights would probably include acquisitions of new companies, undertaking of significant new debts or significant new capital improvement programs, or termination of CEO or other named top executives by the new buyer/owner of the company.

The more rights of consent, which may be built into the stock agreement structure for protection of the minority shareholder, the better.

Two years ago our firm sold 75% of a material handling company for $13 million. We had a buy/sell with the new parent corporation, which provided that $3 million of this price was to be paid to our seller in a note, over a five year time period. The deal prohibited the new owners from doing further add-on acquisitions, until the note was repaid in full.

Less than a year after the transaction, the buyer developed strong interest in a possible add-on acquisition. Our client was uncomfortable adding risk to the deal, and the new owner's banks wanted our client's note receivable to become subordinate to their new debt for the acquisition. We ended up making a deal to leave the $3 million note in place, only if the buyer would first pay us for purchase in full of our remaining 25% equity, at a price based on the now higher current earnings level of the acquired company. Our client received $7.5 million for his last 25% equity share, just over one year after selling his first 75% for $13 million. Our client remained at risk for his $3 million note, but aggregate pricing was now adequate in overall proceeds, to make such risk very acceptable.

In cases where the buy/sell agreement is between non-majority other shareholders (management key people, or strategic corporate investors), often any number of other more varied formulae may be used for pricing. They might include a put/call provision, allowing one shareholder to make an offer to another, where the other must either accept that offer or beat it by some specified dollar amount, within a short time frame (i.e., 30–90 days). Another possible pricing mechanism might include an "insider auction provision," where shareholders agree to a cross-auction at a specified future date. The "suicide" provision is another fast and highly decisive mechanism, which tends to avoid frivolous discussions of sale. With a suicide provision, any shareholder is permitted to put forth an offer to purchase at his estimated value pricing, generally with a simultaneous deposit to indicate certainty of financial capability and commitment to carry through. The other shareholder can then either accept such offer, or decline it, and instead pay the same price to the would-be buyer.)

These are only a few of the more creative ways to provide a workable buy/sell program, but they can be an absolutely critical part to design of a good shareholder agreement.

Closing Day

AS THE TRANSACTION nears close, that final event, and the way buyer and seller announce it to staff and to the world at large, can offer tremendous help to a strong start for the new ownership group and for the future of the company. When the announcement is made it is best for buyer and seller to stand shoulder-to-shoulder together as they tell staff what change has occurred, and what such change will mean to their futures.

We have very seldom had any key people eliminated with a sale. If buyers pay well for the transaction, they want to KEEP the people who have brought the company to where it is. (If there are some who have been "outgrown" by the company, they may face pressure as new owners watch their performance, but if that does occur it is usually something that was destined to come at some time anyway—just as a natural part of growth and evolution of the company.)

Before closing day, buyer and seller need to identify the sensitive points for the announcement (key management staff, major customers, sometimes critical suppliers), and develop an agreed and well orchestrated plan to ensure positive and timely communication to key players, immediately post close. There may be a small handful of important members who need to be contacted individually before a general announcement to staff. Usually all critical individuals can be reached in a day or a couple of days at most, and this can smooth the transition process immeasurably.

CHAPTER 3

Tricks of the Trade

Why Sellers Sell

MOST PEOPLE ASSUME that the vast majority of business owners who sell are probably a little over 60 years old, with no obvious family successor/CEO, and are contemplating retirement. Years of experience have clearly proven to us that this is not the most common profile. There are far more sellers of strong companies who are in their 40s. They have been successful and have grown their businesses well, but one day they decide they would prefer to cash in their chips and let someone else take the business onward to its next phase.

Owners become tired of the risk and hassle of business ownership. With each new change, and at each new plateau, they constantly face the need for new skills, more people, and improved capital infrastructure.

Often they begin to feel like their closest partners are the IRS, the DOL, and the EPA. Business owners tend to appreciate Murphy's Law of Business Regulation: *"For every business action there is an equal and opposite government program."* Owners also become intensely frustrated with the raw magnitude of taxes they find themselves paying—usually well over 50%. They feel that they keep so little of their net profit, that perhaps it just isn't worth it. As one of my clients put it, *"I think I've finally figured out the whole fundamental idea of government. Here it is: if enough people get together and act in concert, they can take your stuff and not pay for it."* Waste in government is, alas, a fact of life, and that too tends to drive business people crazy. (*"A billion here, a billion there—pretty soon you're talking real money."*—Senator Everett Dirkson.)

We have often joked that the tax system is a great boon to our business, because of the frustration it creates among business owners. In reality, there is a healthy dose of serious truth to that.

Another element to owner desire for change relates to how a business owner's job function tends to evolve. Often the talents that helped them most in their early years are far distant from the skills required to handle their now more mature company. As a result, they find themselves doing more of what they least like. This may actually be one of the most intense motivators for sale. Owners are often shy about admitting this as a part of their reason for considering sale, but they shouldn't be. It's a viable and understandable rationale.

Whatever your motives, buyers need to hear, understand, and believe in your reason for sale. If you say, "I no longer have fun in the business, because I have become an administrator, instead of a salesman (or engineer, or whatever), buyers like that. They think perhaps there is an opportunity for them to do the administrative jobs, while you return to your sweet spot—surely a win/win!

If you say, "I've done well but I'm not sure that I have the expertise administratively to take the company to its next level," the buyer can understand that. Frankly, most buyers react to that very positively, because they think they **can** handle the next leg of growth.

Several years ago I spoke about private company sales at a business symposium for middle market owners. The event was an annual affair, and drew a wide range of business types. After my talk, I was queried by a 47-year-old man who had been trying to sell his business for almost a year.

He explained that he wanted to sell because he was afraid that his product was going to become obsolete. He manufactured a patented device used by most of the oil drilling operations around the world. His market penetration was outstanding, and yet he worried, because alternative products were consistently being tried in attempt to replace his product at a lesser cost. He told me that this single issue was his most vulnerable point in the courtship of buyers. He asked how I would suggest he deal with it.

I suggested, first of all, that he use his position effectively in identifying best buyers. He had a proprietary product, which gave him solid positioning in a market which others would want to access. Most of the drilling operations worldwide used his product. If he could identify buyers who longed for entry into those drilling equipment markets, then even just a few years of success by his side, with a buyer adding more product offerings, could be immensely valuable.

Secondly, I suggested that he consider being absolutely forthright about his insecurity. Telling a would-be buyer that he had a golden spot or nitch, which for years had been much coveted by his competitors, might not be such a bad thing. Admitting that he wasn't able to broaden his product range to fully capitalize on his customer base could actually entice buyers. For the right buyer, this opportunity could provide enough very fast value to make the ongoing competitive risk quite palatable.

One year later I did a return guest speaker spot at the same event. The same business owner was there once again, and he sought me out afterward to thank me, and to tell me what a great difference the more direct approach had made in his efforts to sell. He said in his initial efforts, before last year's seminar, he had met with at least ten buyers and had received no real offers. He went on to say that in the sixty days after our chat, three out of four new buyers he had talked with had made offers to buy his company. He generously gave much credit to his improvement in mindset and his more straightforward discussion approach, resulting from our talk. He closed a very successful deal, and he was enormously pleased.

There is one final very popular and very compelling reason why owners become bold enough to sell. They decide it's time to give more attention to their families and the things that bring them joy in life.

Building a business is highly absorbing enterprise. It requires tremendous focus, time, and energy, sometimes at the cost of neglect to other areas of our lives. Often after a business owner has spent ten years or more at such effort, he begins to realize that opportunities for certain family and personal pleasures slip away with the passage of time.

> *Years ago we worked with a client who had decided to sell because his wife had cancer, and he wanted to have more time with her. We got his sale done in about four and a half months, which was excellent under the circumstances, and he went on to have a great time with his wife for almost two more years, when she succumbed to the cancer. I had a discussion with him during a holiday weekend about six months later. He told me his wife had been begging him to sell the business for probably five years before he called us. He said that, in retrospect, the memories which the two of them had created in their last two years together would pay greater dividends for the rest of his life, than all of his investment of the very large sum of cash he had achieved in sale.*

Personal or family needs are an entirely viable reason to contemplate exit from your business.

Competition

WHEN THE TIME comes for serious move toward sale of your company, do not start by giving a smiling nod to the next chance caller to inquire about possible purchase. This is a grave mistake and yet it happens amazingly often. You will not find the optimum buyer by chance. Give yourself at least the possibility of achieving optimal outcome by getting the mechanics of the selling process under control.

Plan the process. Guard confidentiality. Consider potential best buyers carefully. Prepare savory and meticulously accurate information for presentation to buyers. Lastly—and most importantly of all—create COMPETITION.

In order to achieve maximum pricing, there is no single element in the selling process more important than the creation and maintenance of competition. There is a fundamental truth here that every seller needs to appreciate. Competitive pressure always causes buyers to pay more. That is so critical, so fundamental, and so important to success ... Let me repeat it:

COMPETITIVE PRESSURE ALWAYS CAUSES BUYERS TO PAY MORE.

Buyers have a responsibility to buy as economically as possible, regardless of their need or desire for the purchase. They will only pay maximum price if they must, in order to capture the deal. This is the natural law of a free economy at work. Market price governs.

Al Capone once said, "You can get more with a kind word and a gun, than with a kind word alone." Competitive pressure pushes pricing to its maximum.

If the business combination is one of those lovely fits where one plus one equals three, who in fact will get the benefit of the "extra" one? The buyer will not pay that extra benefit to the seller simply to be a nice guy. If the seller isn't courting other competitive suitors at the same time, the astute buyer will perceive that, and will offer only the minimum necessary to secure the deal. The buyer CAN pay more, in a 1+1=3 situation, but generally the buyer WILL pay more only if market competition forces him to do so, in order to win the deal.

There is no obligation, just because the buyer can make more money with your business than you can, for him to pay you for that synergy. The buyer will feel that the synergy fairly belongs to him— not you.

Several years ago a perspective client came to us with an offer in hand to buy his company for $10 million. The owner had a feeling that the price was too low, but wasn't sure what his company was worth. We also were uncertain about precise value, *but the company was growing tremendously, was extremely well run, and was in a nice niche which we knew many buyers would be excited about. In this particular instance, the difficulty of the engagement was greatly magnified by the fact that our client really preferred to sell to the original perspective buyer, and was reluctant to let others bid. We took the engagement only on the condition that we would be allowed to court alternative buyers, although we still knew full well that our client strongly preferred and hoped to see a deal consummated with the original suitor. We were confident that we could improve price, but were not certain that the original buyer would rise to the occasion.*

Upon accepting the engagement, we immediately made it clear to the buyer that we were talking also to alternative suitors, and that the only way to close the deal without our full-blown courtship of competitive bids was to increase purchase price significantly. In less than thirty days the original buyer increased his proposal from $10 million to $25 million in cash at closing, plus another $15 million in potential additional price, if certain prospective targets were met. The deal closed in sixty days. (Happily, the company has since gone on to exceed every financial target, and both buyer and seller remain pleased.)

Even for a perfect acquisition fit, the buyer will not pay premium price unless absolutely necessary. Competition pushes pricing to maximum.

Intermediary Shield

IS IT NECESSARY, when moving to sell your business, to hire an intermediary, or an investment banking firm, or a business broker? Certainly a business can be sold by the owner directly, but generally it's not prudent.

The skilled intermediary can bring tools and techniques to the negotiating process, which you alone can't access. The professional intermediary will have experience that makes a world of difference. It's like having a machine gun instead of a 22-caliber rifle. The number of techniques at the disposal of the professional will be many times greater, readily at hand, and accessible many times faster, simply because he or she has been there before.

Let's talk specifics. An intermediary can say things about you or your company that simply would not come off as well if said by you directly. *It's like telling a perspective blind date for a friend why they might enjoy the company of your friend. "He's intelligent, he has a great sense of humor, and he's really handsome!" If your friend called the perspective date and said, "I'm intelligent, I have a great sense of humor, and I'm really handsome," it would be far less credible. It simply doesn't work.*

Even the bad news passes through easily with an intermediary. In fact, with the right spin, bad news can actually be used to the seller's advantage. "The owner is a brilliant guy, but quite frankly, he's an engineer. The people-side of this business isn't his strength. If you, buyer, can bring in the people skills needed, this company could soar!" To the buyer with team building as a major strength, this is the perfect fit. They can let the seller remain, doing what he is really great at, using his talents to the maximum. The right buyer may literally be likely to triple profitability with minimum additional cost, by fitting their strengths into the precise weaknesses of the seller.

The middleman also gives you the time to think during the course of negotiations. He makes the first foray on all proposals. You get to hear, consider, and strategize about your response before the buyer sees or hears it. You run no risk of knee-jerk frustration, of deal-killing anger, or (at the opposite end of the spectrum) of showing excess glee or relief when a good thing happens. You avoid showing your hand.

When trying to work through a knotty problem, your intermediary can safely float trial balloons. "I have an idea. I'm not sure that my client will go for it, but it seems to me that it could get us most of the way there—if it works for you. ...."

The intermediary can take the hard stance on an issue, and still leave room to back down if necessary. "I'm almost positive this isn't going to work for my client. I will run it by them, if you tell me I must, but I think it really makes better sense for us both to try to find some other solution. How would you feel about ..."

Any time you inject competition among buyers, an independent professional can help enormously to keep an unbiased tone to the competitive nature of discussions. The owner is not perceived as the hard-nosed "it's-all-about-the-money" bad guy. It's the intermediary's stated job to produce the best and highest offer for the company. He isn't bad for creating a horse race. It's his job.

The intermediary may temper his price focus slightly, but buyers know and understand that he will be and should be the guardian of price. He might say, "It's not entirely a pricing issue. Given reasonably close proposals, I know the owner would give up some sales price to do what he feels is best for the people and the company long term. However, that doesn't mean that money is not a factor. It's my job to ensure that the finalists in this process are all at least reasonably close to a solid market value."

Buyers will understand that the owner has a responsibility to his family and/or to other shareholders to cash in reasonably well. If a buyer is within spitting distance on price, it's reasonable for buyers to try to sell their proposal on the basis of non-price intangibles. However, even the world's greatest buyer in terms of the intangibles (culture, attitude, and fit) doesn't expect to get by with offering substantially less than what the company is worth, if there is a professional intermediary involved.

There are also many points along the way where the buyer too is happy to have an intermediary sounding board. The buyer may want to make the point that the company's plant is a mess. He would hesitate to tell the seller directly, for fear of insulting him, but perhaps it's seriously bothering him, and he's worried about EPA, safety, or other issues as a result. The intermediary gives him a way to lay out his concerns, and to more safely explore what might be done to increase his comfort level about the problem. An experienced and cool third party will hear, understand, and think clearly about creative approaches to explore the problem, and reasonably resolve it.

Lastly, the intermediary usually has more staying power than the owner would in the selling process. The owner has two principal issues that lessen his deal "endurance." **(1)** The owner has a business to manage. Frankly, if the company doesn't do well on a steady and continuous basis as it approaches sale, all else is for naught. It is very hard to sell a business while paying strong attention at the same time to the running of that business. **(2)** The owner has a much higher personal emotional stake in the sale, and his involvement is, accordingly, far more intense and far more exhausting. When a buyer steps back with a "no thanks" after hundreds of hours of courtship, it can be very disheartening, and very tempting to give up. The professional intermediary realizes that setbacks are all just part of the game. The professional takes setbacks in stride and quickly retrenches for another approach. The best of the best have amazing tenacity and resiliency.

There is a Chinese proverb that we often quote at my firm. *"The person who says it cannot be done should not interrupt the person doing it."*

All told there are an enormous number of middleman moves that a smart independent professional can make most effectively. He must be experienced, highly skilled, and very much in tune with what the owner will want in order to be optimally effective. Those things given, the use of an intermediary can triple the likelihood of eventual success in sale.

Silence is Golden

EVERYONE HAS HEARD the old adage "protect the goose which lays the golden eggs." In the world of mergers and acquisitions, the goose is the business to be sold. Protecting it means, to a large extent, jealously preserving confidentiality during the selling process.

Most business owners instinctively know this. Customer relationships are critical, and in a competitive environment, may be fragile. If your customers hear that you are considering selling your company, will they immediately turn to alternative vendors? Probably not, but maybe... and maybe is enough to be dangerous. The larger the business is, the less sensitivity here, but there is always some. Customers worry about key suppliers facing ownership transition. They fear that the people they deal with may change. They fear that the direction or focus of the company may change. They seek not to be dependent upon any vendor, but especially not upon a vendor who may be distracted or disoriented by ownership changes. They seldom abandon a vendor for these reasons, but they certainly might seek to ensure that they have a relationship with an alternative source—just in case.

The second area of exposure to damage from non-confidentiality involves employees. The key people (the best people) in any organization are always desirable in a competitive marketplace. People naturally feel insecure in times of ownership transition. If your people learn that you are considering sale, will they immediately put their resumes on the street? Probably not, but the best ones don't need to. Perhaps they just react a tad differently the next time they are approached by a would-be employer or headhunter. It may be just that little bit of added insecurity about the future that causes them to say, "I really don't know what will happen in the next year. Maybe it is time for me to at least listen to other opportunities."

Even the rank and file staff members will be dramatically less efficient with rumor mill gossip about a possible sale as a topic of discussion. It's a tremendously interesting and distracting kind of news. It's an alarming prospect to many. Employee worry and speculation can only harm an employee's productivity, and certainly will do nothing to ease the transition post sale.

In spite of all of these very just and reasonable concerns, you simply can't sell a company without telling someone that it's for sale. *It's like winking at a woman (or man) in the dark. If you're the only one who knows what you have in mind, you won't get anywhere.*

How, then, does one protect confidentiality during the selling process? First, the owner should have virtually no conversations with possible buyers without a carefully drawn nondisclosure agreement in place. From the very first phone call, there is exposure. The buyer must be made to understand immediately that any conversations must be held in the strictest confidence, and that he is expected to sign a legally binding nondisclosure commitment before any discussions proceed.

Owners often feel that the formal confidentiality agreement is not needed until financial statement details are shared. Not so! The first verbal acknowledgment that you might consider sale at all is a risk, and needs to be covered immediately.

We have heard countless stories of breaches in confidentiality in the very earliest stages that caused serious problems. The excited potential buyer gets a firm "maybe" from the seller, and is enthusiastic. Two hours later he opens a sales meeting with, "Guess who we may be buying?" The damage is done. From there it's a short hop to customers and employees.

The nondisclosure agreement used by our firm identifies the client number, instead of the name. Thus the buyer does not know the identity of the seller until after he signs the nondisclosure agreement. This is clearly the safest route.

Another important benefit from carefully guarding confidentiality is the enhancement of buyer appetite. When our firm goes through our typical process of selling a company, we do a lot of research early on to be sure we have the "right" buyers. As we begin approaching those buyers, we let them know up front that we are careful about selecting only the best fitting buyers, and that the opportunity will not be presented to a large number of prospects.

This approach does two important things:

It encourages the buyer to respect and guard the information more carefully, both because the buyer knows it would be easy to trace any confidentiality leak, due to the smaller number of players, and because the buyer PREFERS to keep the deal quiet so that more buyers won't hear about the opportunity and join in the competitive hunt.

Also, there is an odd sort of psychological impact to keeping the field of buyers narrow. It's more exciting for buyers to know there are fewer contenders. Even though the few we talk with are, we hope, the best and toughest competitive contenders for the deal, the buyer still likes the opportunity better because he's one of a small number.

If you can't get people to listen any other way, tell them it's confidential. **Frighteningly true.**

Buyers—360 Degrees

THE MAJORITY OF business owners who come to us think that they know, at the outset, who their best buyers will be. Ninety percent of the time, they are wrong.

Often the buyer most readily thought of is the head-to-head competitor, who has been there, in competition, for many years. The business owner may also be excited about the long time suitor who has religiously called every couple of years for a decade. The owner quickly jots down his short list and thinks those are the likely best buyers.

Although the short list contenders often do want to look, they are rarely, in the end, the most generous buyers.

Direct competitors in many cases can't pay the premium price, because they actually have less to gain. They are already established in similar markets. They know the supply chains. They already compete for the same customers. They may even have a very similar distribution network. It's true that they would always like to knock out a competitor, and they would be a buyer almost certainly at the right price. However, their right price may be a bargain price that the seller never would or should accept.

The overt long-time chaser, who has been calling to probe about possible sale for years, is typically an expert shopper. He keeps his wish list in the file, and methodically follows up to try to be at the right place at the right time. To the seller he is the easy solution. Also, because of his steadfast attention, the seller may think he's the one most likely to pay well. After all, he has been calling for years. Alas, though, this buyer is probably a very seasoned veteran who will quietly bide his time and buy right or not buy at all. He has all the time in the world and is under no pressure to get your deal done.

So where do the best buyers come from? Oh, what a joy to explore!

My grandma used to say, "Honey, everybody has their own unique set of interests. If we all liked the same thing, the whole world would be after your grandpa."

Buyers come from every direction—a full 360 degrees—and then above and below as well! They may be companies which provide goods or services similar to yours, but who need an adjacent product or service to round out their offering. They may be companies which understand your product well, but who don't yet have an entry to your particular universe of customers. They may be companies that need your geography. They may be companies which are almost like yours, but whose greatest strength matches itself perfectly to your greatest weakness.

Good buyers inevitably pop up in multiple segments. The smart seller methodically investigates all that he can actively ferret out, before deciding who he will invite to look at his company.

Is that a complicated task? Absolutely. Our firm typically spends hundreds of man-hours just sorting out and exploring our best five to ten categories of buyers, for any single client seller. As intermediaries, it is our job to find out who is buying whom and why. We segment buyers into baskets by likely synergy, or fit. Then we identify perhaps the top ten in each category to call to probe further.

There are some tasks in business that you do knowing full well that 90% of your effort will be wasted. Perhaps only 10% has value. You do the 90% anyway because FINDING the premium 10% is absolutely worth it. Buyer investigation during the process of selling a business is one of those tasks.

We talk individually to hundreds of potential buyers in a single sale engagement. We ask about their acquisition interests. We ask how important growth is to their business plan, and how likely it is that such growth will be through acquisition. We ask what businesses they've purchased in the past year. We ask what their rules of thumb are for valuing and pricing the businesses that they buy.

We ask what profitability level they judge to be good performance, and what growth levels they see as desirable and credible. We ask what key other attributes of a business they see as the hot buttons that make an acquisition candidate particularly desirable. We ask what they prefer to avoid in the businesses they buy. We learn everything possible about the buyer desires and targets.

> *A few years ago we were in the process of early buyer exploration for a sale engagement, when we encountered two especially eager buyers interested in our client. Both told us that their companies were highly acquisitive, and further that their personal, individual job success actually was heavily dependent upon getting a number of acquisitions done in the year. Great news! Our favorite kind of buyers! These two suitors ended up pushing the price point to an astounding high. The winner was a hero to his company, and we were heroes to our client. Happy day.*

Will buyers really talk openly about their acquisition needs and interests? Absolutely. There is nothing a buyer likes better than to be approached by someone with a thorough understanding of what they want, who is able to say, "I have a perfect acquisition candidate for you."

It is far easier for a well-known, bonafide intermediary to ask these questions than it would be for the seller to do so directly. Information would likely be tainted if the prospective buyer knew that he was speaking to the seller directly. However, only the foolish seller would attempt the hundreds of hours to take on a buyer-screening task directly. Always hire a professional. Then make sure they test every angle of fit you can identify. The big win doesn't usually come from the most obvious player.

Honesty Pays

IT PAYS, INEVITABLY and invariably, to be forthright in presentation of information about your company to a prospective buyer. Forthright does not mean that you must necessarily share all levels of detail. There may be details that you need to withhold in the interests of protecting confidentiality. For those issues, you simply need to say, "We don't wish to provide that information now." Thus, you remain forthright, even when you do refuse to provide information.

With all information that you **are** willing to share, be scrupulously honest. When we take on any engagement, we warn perspective clients that if they aren't comfortable with being forthright, they won't like us. We believe that and live by it—and we are absolutely comfortable that such belief integrates perfectly with a clear profit motive. Superb deals always come from a foundation of truth. Only the most secure buyer will have the courage to push pricing to the maximum. Giving truth **allows** buyers to be bold.

Also, bad news can be far more effectively dealt with in the earlier stages of discussions. To pretend that a problem doesn't exist is a fool-hardy deception. Problems are far less important or dangerous when full and fair disclosure is made up front, in a forthright manner. Often the buyer will have no adverse response to the issue whatsoever. In fact, in many cases the buyer will see the problem or weakness as an opportunity for substantive improvement. Particularly in areas where the correction seems relatively easy, the buyer may actually see the potential improvement as low hanging fruit, or fast and easy money to be made post-closing.

> *Several years ago we were representing an outstanding equipment manufacturer in sale. The company had a technically superior product and their growth had been strong and steady, in spite of literally zero sales force. When perspective buyers asked about the company's selling process and people, they explained that virtually all of their growth had been through a constant stream of customers finding them. Unlike our client, competitors in their industry had smooth and polished sales mechanisms to fuel growth. With every buyer, our client was modest, apologetic, and even somewhat embarrassed when the discussion turned to the topic of sales systems. Buyers appreciated such openness about the weakness, and saw opportunity in the solution. Virtually every suitor for the company walked away from the client's shy discussion of this topic with a definite increase in appetite. We sold the company for a superb price.*

Buyers of companies control substantial amounts of cash, and are generally highly responsible and bright people. *(A fool and his money are ... a rare combination.)* If sale is being considered because of some serious problem pending, the buyer is very likely to ask the right question to unearth the problem. Furthermore, even if they don't unearth the problem in the natural course of events, if it's important, it should be disclosed. Lack of disclosure regarding a material problem will inevitably violate some representation or warranty which will be required in the purchase agreement before the deal is finalized.

If the purchase agreement doesn't explicitly seek information on the specific matter itself, it will, at a minimum, require the seller's representation that he has fairly disclosed any material, potentially adverse matters pending. If you, as a seller, expect to keep the proceeds of sale, it helps to have come by them honestly.

Think Big

One of the most critical elements to outstanding deal making is the ability to think big. Thinking big doesn't mean just setting a big target price. It means *believing in value*.

PERIODICALLY AT MY firm we have strategy sessions to discuss deal status and to brainstorm about trouble spots. Inevitably, one of the most valuable elements of such strategy sessions lies in our ability to help one another build enthusiasm, and redouble our own belief in the worth of our clients. We talk about what it is about each company that has sparkle and sizzle, from varied individual perspectives. Each contributed spark of enthusiasm creates ideas for the team, and nurtures our excitement about the client.

When we have the true heartfelt conviction that the company we're selling is a wonderful find, it shows. It leaks out in our tone of voice, in our choice of words, and in the gleam in our eye. Our enthusiasm and conviction is contagious to buyers. We aggressively pressure for great prices when we believe that we **deserve** great prices.

Please don't misunderstand this advice. I am not advocating total lack of realism. There is a time for everything. Before you begin, look realistically and even skeptically at your position. Think hard. Be tough on yourself. Be realistic about your flaws and risks, and build counter information to deal with problem spots.

However, when all of that is done, before buyer encounters begin, pause, take a deep breath, and bask in thoughts of your strengths.

I once gave this advice to a client, who responded by telling me that my advice was similar to words of wisdom he had heard from a senator friend of his. The senator told him that the key to happiness is the ability to convincingly delude ourselves. I was hoping for a more heartfelt response, but my client was a very tired business owner.

Master the art of "psyching up" to a THINK BIG mentality. There is one other tremendous benefit to this mental preparation. Sometimes, thankfully, it happens that buyers exceed our fondest dreams. When that occurs it is critical to internalize such good fortune and become comfortable with it immediately. The transaction instantly has a new threshold. The business has proven to be worth this lovely new amount. The market has spoken. Raise your sites. Get comfortable quickly with your newly elevated status, and push for continuing improvement with each additional step forward.

That is how home runs happen.

Exclusivity

IN ORDER TO keep the pressure of competition as tightly drawn as possible, sellers need to avoid entering into an exclusive dealings commitment for as long as possible. Buyers will push for speed. They will submit an agreement for seller acceptance with a tight time deadline to pressure the seller into speedy acceptance. *As a client of mine once put it, "I love deadlines. I like the whooshing sound they make as they fly by."*

If you have healthy competition, understand that pressure for speed is a sign of sincere interest, but don't be tempted to act rashly.

Smart buyers will always offer a letter of intent very early with an exclusive dealings clause, or a "stop-shop." Such a clause requires that the seller agree to cease discussions with alternative buyers. Buyer and seller are thus engaged to be married. As the seller is asked to make this commitment, the buyer in turn makes a pledge at the same time, but usually it's a much less onerous pledge. The buyer, in the letter of intent, typically says that he intends to buy the company at X price. He agrees with all good speed to work through getting the purchase done, including drafting documents, completing due diligence investigations, and obtaining financing. However, the buyer usually may back out at any time if something doesn't work out to his satisfaction.

Obviously, this is a pretty one-sided commitment, and thus is a bad deal for the seller. The buyer will argue that it's fair and reasonable, and that it's a necessary concession to make it reasonably safe and economical for him to incur the expense for the next phase of purchase investigation.

In our selling efforts we try very hard not to accept a stop-shop, unless or until the buyer is ready to put down a substantial non-refundable deposit. Buyers don't like that, but they will live with it if they must. Either we work out all of the important terms, get these terms in writing, and mutually commit to go forward (barring fraud or catastrophic events) or the buyer must be willing to move forward without securing our commitment to exclusivity.

Additionally, we always make sure that buyers we deal with know that they are not the only ones at the table. As a result, our deals finish more quickly, and with very little backsliding, either in dollar pricing or key terms.

Statistically, a majority of deals in the United States that progress to the letter of intent stage never make it to close. Even for those that do eventually close, all too many may do so only after late-stage price reductions by the buyer. If the seller has narrowed the field down to one buyer, he has little power to fight back when the buyer reduces price. He can either accept the reduction, or face the risk and hassle of going back to the market to start over.

When a seller has accepted a deal, and has told alternative buyers that he has done so, he appears to be severely weakened if he then later comes back to say he is available again. Other buyers naturally wonder what went wrong. What did the original buyer learn that made him back out? The seller is in a vastly improved position with alternative suitors if he has not told them of his initial failed attempt.

Some years ago we accepted a letter of intent from a buyer, choosing his company over about a dozen alternative suitors. Half way through his due diligence, this buyer demanded interviews with all management staff. Our client was very sensitive to confidentiality, and interviews with management were clearly prohibited by the letter of intent. Without such interviews, however, the bank was going to withdraw financing support, and the buyer would be unable to consummate. We let the buyer withdraw and we took the company back to market, contacting the entire cadre of suitors who had previously submitted bids. Not one of those suitors wanted to re-initiate an offer. They all felt insecure about the fact that we had chosen a buyer, but that the chosen buyer was not now moving forward. We ended up re-marketing the company again to all new buyers. In the end we closed at an even better price—but it took us and additional five months of effort and hundreds of hours to find, court and complete negotiations with the new buyers. A failed transaction can be costly.

In summary: Avoid exclusivity for as long possible. Seek to always court more than one competitive buyer. Keep multiple competitors warm and active, running a side-by-side course until very close to the end, and orchestrate completion to occur quickly after a firm commitment is made.

"Asking" Price

AS A COMPANY proceeds to market, the first question almost every buyer will ask is, "What does the owner want for the company?" Almost all professional sellers of businesses refuse to set price. Instead, they require the buyer to set their own price.

Buyers will naturally resist going first, if at all possible. It is uncomfortable. If they start too high, they may pay far more than they otherwise would have had to. If they start too low, they may be dismissed as "bottom-fishers," not worthy of talking to.

In spite of the clear strategic advantages to making the buyer set price, sellers are often very nervous about refusing to give an "asking" price. They feel rude or disingenuous in not being willing to tell prospective buyers what their expectations are. Further, the buyer may react unhappily or angrily, and exert a great deal of pressure to induce the seller to be more "candid." The seller may be afraid that he will lose a good prospect, and feel almost compelled to throw out a number.

Whoever "starts" the pricing process faces risk. If the seller gives a price, and it is far above the buyer's expectations, the buyer will be annoyed, feeling that the seller is unreasonable and foolish, and the buyer will withdraw. If the seller's price is lower than anticipated, he will never even know of his error. The buyer will still complain that the price stated is too high. He will moan and fume, and then move forward to get the seller to drop a little more. If he says, "okay—done," the seller would clearly KNOW that his price was too low. Thus, by stating price, all the seller has achieved is the setting of a solid cap on what he might get for his company.

There is no rule, no ethic, no responsibility **whatsoever**, for the seller to pre-set the pricing. Buyers are perfectly capable of competitively venturing price points. Experienced and more sophisticated buyers are quite accustomed to it. They will still need to feel competitive pressure to make them willing to push their offering price to something near their high end, but they can and will respond.

The payoff for proper handling of the pricing question can be tremendous. We are experienced sellers, having seen pricing on literally hundreds of transactions over the years. Still, we can be and often are surprised. When competition is fierce, it is not uncommon for a few buyers to come in at literally double the pricing of the median on a deal.

The potential cost of error in this area is simply too enormous to dismiss. It pays to hang tough and **make** the buyer set the price.

The Right Resources: Intermediaries

IN SELLING A company, it is absolutely critical, if you are to maximize results, to get the right team of resources working for you. The team here includes the intermediary who will represent you overall, the attorney who will handle document negotiations, the CPA who will coach your team on the tax aspects of the transaction, and the internal resources who will support the gathering of necessary information, and may even be involved in late-stage interviews with prospective buyers.

The intermediary will be the one who finds your buyers, who makes the initial approaches to these buyers, who responds to buyer inquiries and proposals, and who ushers the entire process along to fruition. It's a critical job. This person will make the most of, or, if unsuccessful, the least of your life's work. It's a scary thing to consider handing over such immense responsibility to someone you hardly know.

If you don't give this task to someone specifically skilled and practiced in this very thing, you are absolutely guaranteed to achieve lesser results. Neither your attorney, nor your CPA, nor your COO, nor your lifelong smart business person pal will even come close to the capabilities of a well qualified professional. A professional firm will spend hundreds of hours focused upon this one task for you. It is their job. They won't be interrupted by a separate workload to distract them, and they won't be losing a client when they successfully complete your sale. They exist to sell companies. This job is far too important to place in the hands of someone for whom it's a sideline. You deserve to be the main event.

Normally business intermediaries will not be people you know and have worked with before. If all they do is sell businesses, you probably have not needed their services before. So how do you know they are good?

Begin with selecting a firm that focuses entirely upon buy and sell transactions. There are hundreds of consultants, and assorted business advisors who have some experience, but who do other things as well. They will not be as competent, as well staffed, or as experienced as the specialist.

You need an intermediary whose fundamental **livelihood** depends upon successful closings. If your deal is only supplemental income to a separate core business, it will not receive the same intense dedication. *It's a little like bacon and eggs. The hens are involved, but the pigs are committed.*

Check references. It's necessary and prudent to check that they have, in fact, done a competent job for other business sellers. An intermediary's clients were themselves business owners cashing in on a life's work, just like you. They will usually talk with honesty and forthrightness to the reference contacts that call them.

It is worth the time and trouble to make those phone calls. I'm often amazed to be hired by business owners who haven't spoken to any of our references. Although we're naturally honored to have such trust, this seems incredibly dangerous to me.

As you study an intermediary's proposed fee schedule, it is also important to seek someone who will design a strong incentive system that you like. There is no better insurance for keeping someone aggressively working on your side than to be sure they are paid very well if, and only if, they succeed for you.

A part of your selection decision will be, and should be, dependant upon your personal chemistry with the lead person or people. Be sure that you get acquainted with the key people who will be personally handling your transaction. You will be depending upon them for a very important job. You must be able to make your needs and wishes clearly known to them, and you must be able to understand their communications back to you.

Lastly, always ask about success rates for any intermediary you consider. Although no one will be 100% successful, the best can come pretty close.

The Right Resources: Legal Counsel

IN A SALE transaction, the legal representation you need will probably involve a lead attorney different from the key person with whom
you have historically worked. You need an expert, experienced and
seasoned in business sale transactions. You need a specialist. From
a technical standpoint, your legal counsel will play a critical role, and
you will depend on him in important ways to monitor and control the
purchase agreement. The average purchase agreement is 50–100
pages long, plus exhibits and attachments. It's a complex document,
and your attorney is your bodyguard.

> *A doctor, an engineer and a lawyer were arguing over whose pro-
> fession was the oldest. "On the sixth day, God took one of Adam's
> ribs and created Eve," said the doctor. "So that makes him a sur-
> geon first." "Please," said the engineer. "Before that, God created
> the world from chaos and confusion, so he was first an engineer."
> "Interesting," said the lawyer smugly, "But who do you think
> created the chaos and confusion?"*

In spite of the complexity and the dangers, when choosing the
attorney to guide you through this morass, you need to look for more
than technical genius and protective instinct. To succeed, you must
also screen for the ability to creatively compromise. You want someone who closes deals—not someone who "saves" his client from every
good buyer who comes close. The best are those attorneys who focus
on getting the desired deal done, and who can consistently keep their
egos in check. Ask about track record. Find out how many deals they
have worked on in the past year, and how many have closed, and how
many have failed.

Ask prospective attorneys to talk you through what makes them
successful. Check references. Look for abilities to compromise and
understand the opposing view. Value tenacity, but try to make sure

it's tempered with calmness and with creative problem solving capabilities. If the focus of their discussion is to boast about their "saves" which didn't get to closing, go on to the next candidate.

The best deal attorney I have ever worked with was a very low key, even-tempered technical genius, who was virtually impossible to anger. In spite of his doggedly courteous and mild mannered approach to the other side, he was incredibly tenacious. He invariably knew the documents cold, and came back gently but ever so repeatedly with various alternative approaches to winning his each and every point. When he reached an impasse, he didn't mislead the opposition by acquiescing, but he would back gently off for the moment, saying, "I'm not sure I'm comfortable with that. Perhaps if we move on for now, and leave that issue alone, we'll come to some alternative which can work a little later." By the sixth pass on the same issue, his methodology was apparent, and yet it was still hard to circumvent. Eventually he won eight out of ten points, and he always prevailed on the important ones. Just as importantly, he never, in all of my experience with him, killed a deal.

The great ones never kill the deal. They find creative solutions that minimize risk to their client, but still get the job done. In the end, they always come back to the client with sensible and pragmatic advice about risk and reward.

Deal-killer attorneys quickly draw lines in the sand. They are fast to offer advice that, "everyone does it this way," with the corollary implication that "anything less would be outrageously unfair." Everyone does not do it ANY way. The "always require this" approach is deadly. In mergers and acquisitions there truly are norms and mores, but there is no hard line standard. Every problem has a variety of reasonable solutions if the parties are industrious enough and creative enough to find them.

The Right Resources: CPAs

CPAs HAVE A set of problems and issues in a sale engagement differ-ent from other advisors. Your CPA will, in all probability, lose ongoing annuity revenue when and if you are successfully sold, because the buyer will later switch to his own CPA. You will use your normal CPA for the deal, and you will need his involvement. He will feel that his job is to help and protect you. However, you need to take his advice carefully. Make it clear to him that you do want to successfully sell. If you have a deal that you want to accept, make sure he understands that this is your goal.

I grew up as a CPA. I was an audit partner with one of the then Big Eight CPA firms and spent sixteen years in the practice of public accounting. CPAs are taught early in their careers that their job is to become a hero by saving clients from bad things. When CPAs find themselves in transaction analysis, they gravitate very quickly to the search for hidden evils.

I ran a multi-functional merger and acquisition group for my CPA firm, working with audit, tax, and consulting professionals in various merger and acquisition transactions for clients around the Midwest. Very often we found our professionals "sav-ing" clients from things that our clients really did not want to be saved from.

I once was involved in a $300 million deal that was very nearly killed by a $20,000 tax exposure. The deal was about $70 million better than others that had been proposed, and our client was thrilled. One of our young tax men kept warning of an issue that he was very concerned about, and predicting tax doom to come, as a potential result of this issue. Our client naturally relied on the firm to help him ferret out tax exposures, and was accordingly very worried. Finally, we sat down and undertook the task of defining what the real dollar exposure was for this tax problem.

It was $20,000. Tops. We found out in time to avoid harm, but it was embarrassing.

In my experience as an intermediary, one in four of the CPAs representing our clients has been supportive and great, protecting the client, but consistently keeping their client's end-game objective in mind. Another one in four of the CPAs we have worked with have gone to the other extreme—being absolutely obstructive to any transaction. They obstruct in part because they fear losing a client, but even more importantly because they are generally fearful and mistrusting of any transaction. Often, they can't imagine why their client could possibly want to consider sale in the first place. They imagine that their clients "have it made" because they're earning strong profits. They simply do not understand the sense of risk a business owner often feels. The remaining population of CPAs is typically neutral to slightly resistant, mostly in the name of protectionism.

The right way to get optimal accounting help and advice is to talk to your CPA openly and honestly as the transaction moves forward. CPAs generally are an intensely honest and highly service-oriented lot. Be crystal clear in making your desires and objectives known, and tell them that you want to save tax dollars, you want to understand risks, but you want, in the end, to accomplish sale. Also, you might consider a nice bonus to your CPA at closing, for a job well done. He is losing a client, and he does have to be a bit selfless to really help you to get the job done. Recognize and appreciate that fact, be straight with him in communications, and he will probably try very hard to do the right thing.

The Right Resources: Internal

DURING THE COURSE of sale you will need to accumulate fairly substantial information. Obviously you will need financial statements, which are probably already in hand, but you will need a great deal more as well. There will be questions about financial details and about accounting methodologies. Buyers will want to understand customer concentrations. They will want to understand your markets, trends, and competition. They will want to understand geographic mix, product category mix, mix by salesman or rep, and a wide range of factors relating to the overall revenue environment. They will want to see organization charts, and background on key second tier management, and payroll cost information, and more. They will want data on equipment and facilities and taxes and legal status, and the list goes on.

Much of this data is awkward for an owner to obtain without some internal collaboration, at least with a key financial person. Accordingly, some level of involvement for certain staff may be absolutely necessary.

The owner's primary job during the selling process should be to continue to run the operation well. That may be extremely hard to do with a highly hands-on role in the gathering of information for buyers. Thus extensive owner participation in the information gathering process is probably misspent time.

Often a financial helper can be enlisted without full disclosure of the selling process being contemplated. Many owners gather data for the initial phases of the process explaining that they are exploring value for estate planning or financial planning purposes, and simply avoid any more detailed explanation to assisting staff. Some owners have their CPAs gather data, although that too typically requires some explanation, because the operational information required is generally well beyond the scope of standard audit or tax procedures.

Regardless of the assistance you may need from supporting staff, you will be well advised to keep shared information about the possible sale to a minimum. *I have never met a seller in twenty years who regretted secrecy in the matter of contemplated sale. However, I have met many who regretted sharing too much information.* Be guarded and move slowly in communications with staff.

Golden Parachutes
for Troubled Companies

OUR FIRM HAS made its living for almost twenty years by selling companies—some in great times, at absolute peak moments, and others at moments where they were heading downstream quickly, and fast-approaching the waterfall drop-off to potentially end it all. In the tough moments, owners tend to think, "I just don't feel like I can sell right now, even though I would love to reduce risk. I feel like I really have to wait for an upturn."

So... if it is really bad... if your profits are getting impossible to hold—what should you do?

Protect yourself! Take charge and sell while you, your company, and your employees can still survive!

Facing Facts

The hardest thing for the owner of any down-turning company to face is that the business may not be "fixable" by existing management, or by the kids coming along. It takes great courage and resolve to move decisively to sell before it's too late, but the payoff is two to five times more in value. Business descent inevitably accelerates, like a bicycle on a downhill path without brakes. Just slowing the descent is hard. Turning and coming back to the top is extremely difficult, requiring an owner willing to invest substantial money and time to back the changes needed.

> *We sold a metal stamping company in Chicago several years ago. The owners of the company had been flirting with the possibility of sale for about five years. As times got increasingly tough in their industry, they took on new, large, but not-very-profitable business. They knew it wasn't the most desirable business, and yet they rationalized that surely it did help to "cover costs."*

Finally, they found themselves with a nicely sized company in total revenue that was consistently LOSING money. They finally pulled the trigger and hired us to sell them. Two months after we began the selling process, the company was thrown involuntarily into Chapter 11 bankruptcy, due to actions taken by fearful trade creditors. We continued with our selling efforts, and finally got appointed by the federal bankruptcy judge to continue representing them in sale. We did get it done, and we got enough to pay all of the banks, all of the trade creditors, and a little to the shareholders. The final proceeds were almost $25 million less than we had first estimated five years earlier. That was true in spite of the fact that the federal bankruptcy judge said he had more bond-posted, able bidders in the courtroom on the final day than he had ever seen in this type of proceeding, in his entire life-long career. Thus we did a great job comparatively and competitively, although we brought a disappointingly small amount to our shareholder clients, in comparison to what we would have expected five years earlier. Timing made all the difference.

In the down times, companies suddenly feel the pressure—with great force! The cold, hard fact is that continued overseas pressure, impetus toward consolidation, and sagging industry markets will create difficulty in that hard-fought and expensive effort to attempt the rebound.

TIGHTEN UP

If you're tough minded enough to face reality and to move aggressively to save what you can, begin with a hard look at yourself and a healthy dose of belt tightening. You may have to stop the bleeding just to survive long enough to sell.

Cut every cost you can, to trim down to a firm, solid core. Don't mortgage your future. Keep cognizant of the fact that core assets and good people will be needed for the next step up. However, resist the urge to rationalize or stall. If you have excess people, cut back. Where costs can be pared down, do it. Tighten up! Watch cash flow with the keenest of interest.

Punch service to an all-time high. Look for opportunities to strengthen and lengthen service connections to key customers. Build "partnerships" to enhance customer ties. Add services, such as pre- or post-sale assistance to broaden and secure your tie to your customers.

EXPERT HELP

Without delay, get a process of sale started. Do not pick up the phone and open up dialog with every casual prospective buyer you think of. Your employees will hear and become afraid. Your customers will hear and will begin developing "back up" sources. Be smart, and hire professional help to sell your company. There are dozens of excellent business brokers out there, and they are eager to help.

Moving quickly is tremendously important for the troubled company. *("If you're gonna skate on thin ice, you gotta be FAST!")* Professional help can make an enormous difference.

Be selective. Hire someone who focuses only on the purchase and sale of businesses. Your attorney or CPA may be happy to take the job, but they won't have the focused experience or expertise to do it as well as a specialist. Neither do you. Check references. Look for experience with turn-around sales. Look for intensity and commitment in the firm you hire.

CALM LENDERS AND INVESTORS

Depending upon how distressed your company is, you may have some critical issues looming with banks or with other lenders or investors. Communication often can alleviate enormous tension. Your bank does not want to own your assets. Your investors will not like surprises. Often a well-timed and frank discussion of your recognition of the problem, and the actions that you are taking to correct it, will go far in calming outside pressure.

Usually it pays to tell bankers that you are planning sale. In most distressed situations, bankers are pleased and relieved and will react very supportively. They may grant you a standstill on principal payments, interest, or both. They will, however, want to ensure that when you exit, they get paid off. Thus, if they don't have all assets pledged as collateral, they may seek to tighten up their position. Your intermediary or business broker should be able to help and advise you, and keep financial backers calm.

Whatever the level of proactive disclosure you choose, be scrupulously honest in all communications with lenders and investors. You will be glad to have earned their trust and cooperation in tight moments ahead.

THE CHAPTERS

Three or more creditors can throw a company involuntarily into bankruptcy with legal demand. Alternatively, a company may choose to voluntarily seek Chapter 11 status, to operate on an ongoing basis, while being sold. Chapter 11 is a distinct disadvantage in sale from a marketing view because everyone will know you are weak, and that the company can be purchased for a low price. However, buyers love the "no strings attached" cleanliness of purchase. When they buy through Chapter 11, they are guaranteed clear title, with no exposure whatsoever for liabilities relating to past operations. Also, the Chapter 11 filing does buy time by freezing debts for the prospective seller, and forestalls repayments until matters are resolved. Chapter 7, alternatively, is bankruptcy with the intent to liquidate and close operations. Under Chapter 11 you may achieve some value for ongoing customer relationships, intangibles and goodwill, and a significant core of people may well go on to jobs with the new owner. Under Chapter 7, operations generally cease as soon as practicable, and there is seldom any potential for a goodwill element in sale.

The issues in consideration of bankruptcy election are complex, and far beyond the scope of this chapter. However, if there is any possibility that sale won't result in proceeds adequate to pay off all creditors, and then you, as owner, need to fully understand and consider every alternative.

SO...WHAT MAKES SELLERS COME OUT WELL?

(1) Move early and move quickly—sell before value deteriorates.

(2) Tighten your belt to prevent further value from draining away.

(3) Hire expert professional help.

(4) Be forthright with lenders and investors—you need their cooperation.

(5) Know and study your rights, to protect your assets.

There is an old saying; "You can't really tell who's swimming naked until the tide goes out." If you think that it might be you, stop pretending, for goodness sake! Get while the getting is good, and save your company and your nest egg for the future.

Equity Fund Buyers

THERE HAS BEEN a veritable explosion in the number of equity fund buyers over the past decade, and such buyers generally have become far more competitive and viable in the world of closely held business sales. Our private database of qualified equity funds is now over 2,500, compared to probably around 100 quality firms in the market just fifteen years ago. Additionally, equity funds are pricing their purchases today to compete with strategic buyers. Ten years ago our sellers ended up being sold to private equity funds in about one in ten deals. Today, it's more like half of all deals in the $10 million to $200 million-size segment.

The private equity fund also offers some twists in form and content, which, depending on your circumstances, can be quite appealing to the private business owner.

MANAGEMENT STAYS IN PLACE

The private equity funds want management, and even most long time shareholders, to stay involved with the company. They hope such historically important key people can be part of the company's future, and its growth. Private equity funds don't have a stable of industry experts or other employees that they can move in, to replace your people. If you enjoy your business, but need capital for growth, or simply want to reduce your risk by taking a few chips off of the table, they can offer you a great way to do it!

FINANCIAL INCENTIVE FOR FUTURE GROWTH

The typical equity fund likes to leave anywhere from 10% to maybe a third of ownership in the hands of former shareholders and/or employees. This leaves some of the key operating management with a strong incentive to continue to nourish and support the company. In just a handful of years, we have seen a number of these smaller minority retained pieces become almost as large in value as the original super-majority sold! If you are optimistic about your company's future—particularly if your company gets a bit more capital and some sophisticated advisory guidance, this can be a great way to direct your future.

EVOLVING JOB ROLES FOR SENIOR EXECUTIVE (MORE FUN)

We also see a great many owner executives who are excellent at certain aspects of their business, but not at everything. It's those weak spots that haunt owners and keep them up at night, and they can be the hardest areas for that owner to mend or to develop beyond.

For example, the owner who is a natural born people person—a great boss, and a good salesman—may be weak in financial control issues, or administrative function. (That's not his natural gift, or his personal preference.) Post sale to an equity fund, he has assistance in getting top quality people in place for those jobs, and he becomes free to once again do what he's great at (win/win, for both the seller and the equity fund!)

In spite of all of these supportive and complimentary comments about private equity funds, they are difficult to deal with for private company sale in a few ways. The "cons" of equity fund buyers include the following:

SEEKING SELLER COMMITMENT BEFORE A FIRM "BUY" DECISION

Equity funds are often very aggressive about trying to get the seller "committed" to their deal (the exclusivity commitment, to talk to no other buyers) ASAP. All too often, they only then do the real scrutiny to decide firmly about a deal, and they then may later "back out" or withdraw from the deal. In our firm's first fifteen years of operation, we only had one deal, ever, which proceeded to the point of a letter of intent, but which then failed to close. Since the increased participation of equity funds, we have about a fourth of these deals, which may fall apart before close. (This doesn't mean the seller can't complete a transaction, but it does mean far more time, cost, and effort to finally get done.) The cost to the seller of a failed effort is enormous—both in terms of professional service and support, and in terms of lost alternative buyers.

PRICING DEPENDENT ON DEBT AVAILABILITY AND DEBT COST

Equity funds depend heavily on bank backing, and both the pricing of debt and the raw amount of debt possible will have a major impact on their potential pricing. Additionally, this can slow the process fairly significantly, and, as a result, such funds tend to move more slowly than the average "strategic" buyer.

MORE COMPLEX AND BURDENSOME DUE DILIGENCE

Because the equity funds out in the marketplace will tend to know less about your business than the average strategic competitor, and because they need borrowing capacity to get the deal closed, their due diligence process is often more complex, cumbersome, and time-consuming that what the seller might face from a more knowledgeable industry competitor. Additionally, they also require greater access to employees pre-closing (even requiring advance contracts in some cases).

In summary, equity funds are a new and evolving set of buyers in today's marketplace, and they can be a complex and difficult group to "sort out" for a seller. However, they also offer a whole new range of potential solutions for the private business owner who seeks to reduce risk, and can be an excellent suitor for today's sellers.

International Buy/Sell

OVER THE PAST decade plus, the impact of international acquisitions has been a tremendous force in the buy/sell process. World markets continue to widen and thrive, and the impact is to broaden buyer competition to all-time highs as the trends continue.

Some sellers prefer only to sell to buyers from their home nation. That is fine, and certainly is the seller's right to choose, but even for those with particular determination to stay "close to home." the impact of world market competition is still a beautiful and highly effective force for the benefit of sellers.

International buyers may come from afar because they seek new entries into their target markets. They may come because the seller has greater knowledge and expertise in an area in which they seek to do more in the future. They may become especially strong and competitive in times when their currency is particularly strong, or the target currency is weak. In 2008, for example, many international buyers could acquire more U.S. dollars for a relative bargain price, due to dollar valuations. Thus they could pay MORE dollars for a U.S. acquisition. The international play may also make particular sense when the large and diverse international holding company can blend economic advantages from multiple locations, to create maximum effectiveness and cost efficiency for a blended operation.

> *We sold a U.S. company in 2005 that manufactured packaging for large computer companies. Our client was facing immense competition from the Far East, where many of our client's customers had moved base manufacturing operations. However, our client had certain unique design and distribution mechanisms which allowed them to continue to be powerful in their marketplace, despite the low-cost offshore competition.*
>
> *The final buyer for this client company was an international packaging concern, which blended our U.S. design and distribution talents with their own offshore production capabilities. As an end result of the combination, both the U.S. firm (now focused entirely upon design, service, and distribution) and the offshore production entities grew markedly. Jobs shifted to some extent, but the total job count in the U.S. actually climbed, and our seller client ended a lifetime career of very hard work with a mammoth "win" as he sold.*

Dealing with international buyers introduces somewhat new dynamics to the transaction, and it helps to have advisors familiar with the culture they are courting. It's challenging, but well worthwhile.

Also, the pressure of international competition tends to bring market differences face-to-face as buyers battle to win the acquisition competition. The impact is to produce greater choice for the seller, and greater "balance" among international market conditions, as diverse suitors match wits to enhance worldwide markets.

> *Some years ago we sold a company to a British buyer, who bid a strong and aggressive amount, and won, over much competition. We accepted a letter of intent from that buyer, with the negotiated stipulation that all of our seller's indemnifications regarding reps and warranties made in the deal, could under no circumstances result in any claim against our sellers for more than a maximum of 20% of the deal price. The reps and warranties were fair and reasonable, and our seller's likely exposure was small, because it would have been extremely surprising for any such large contingent issues to arise. However, we still felt that this "cap" was important, just in case. (We always push hard to make sure the seller is reasonably free from any post-sale risk, albeit remote, because we feel that since our seller will not own "upside" potential after the sale, that likewise they should be rid of "downside" exposure.)*
>
> *The buyer's team of attorneys and financial people showed up for the closing, after the transaction had received final approval from their Board the week before. However, at the closing table, they informed us that there was one change in the documents. They said their board had NOT approved the transaction to be done with the cap on indemnifications. (In Europe such caps are rarely if ever done, so they view an unlimited ceiling on such indemnifications as entirely normal.)*
>
> *We told the buyer that we were sorry they had come so far and done so much work on the deal, but we would advise our client to return to alternative offers, instead of accepting such change. It was a tense day, and difficult for both sides, because so much time and effort had already been expended before this point. In the end, however, the buyer agreed to re-insert our provision for the cap on indemnifications.*

This same issue has arisen for us with other European buyers, and we understand and believe that the "no cap" perspective is entirely the norm there. Thus we anticipate the problem. However, if competition involves strong interplay between multinational bidders, this will continue to be an issue, which allows the seller to make a choice, if he wishes to avoid such exposure. International competition pushes hard to allow sellers to select the features they most value, and, over time, tends to press all contenders to a more balanced approach.

Process Timing

THE TOTAL PROCESS of selling a business can take anywhere from two months to two years. Two months is unusual in the extreme, and requires aggressive buyers in hand at the outset, and a willingness on the part of the seller to settle for nominal investigation of possible competitive bidders. On the flip side, two years is extremely slow, and generally would indicate a very real problem.

A reasonable aggregate timeline would be six to ten months. The first two to three months are generally required to gather information about the company for presentation to buyers, and, at the same time, to identify and research who the best buyers may be.

Information to be presented needn't be pulled to an elaborate bound book format in this process. In fact, we recommend strongly against any printed material which cannot be easily updated and revised as the process evolves. However, material does need to be accurate, professional, and presented in a way to very clearly set forth key elements to the deal which make the opportunity attractive to buyers. It is a selling piece, albeit very soft sell.

With respect to buyer search work, the temptation to rely on old biases and assumptions about possible buyers makes it difficult for anyone heavily involved in the company to gain adequate distance to think most creatively. Also, the time to do a quality job in buyer search is extensive. Hired help is worthwhile.

After information is well developed, and you are ready to launch, the early contact stage can be expected to take about another two months. For any given buyer prospect, it may take anywhere from one day to ten days just to get the confidentiality agreement signed, depending on whether or not they require advance legal review before signing. The longer and more complex your confidentiality agreement is, the longer the timeline will be. Although our firm generally uses a very straightforward one page document for this, we have at times had to deal with longer formats, due to a client's attorney preference.

> *On one engagement we had a confidentiality agreement which was a four page, difficult to read document that our side's counsel required of all buyers. In spite of the fact that it really wasn't substantively tougher than others, and didn't require anything unreasonable or onerous, it inevitably went to buyer's counsel before they would sign. It took every buyer at least two weeks to even return the thing to us with first comments. Then we spent a week or two in almost every case negotiating the confidentiality terms in advance of even beginning to talk about our client. A full month was added to our timeline.*

The nondisclosure agreement needs to say that all information, verbal or written, is to be held as confidential. It needs to say that buyer contact to the offices of the company is prohibited. It needs to stipulate that the very fact that the owners are considering the possibility of sale is confidential. If going to a specific and critical competitor, information may need to be limited to named top people only. The agreement should provide for return or destruction of all information on the company at the seller's request. Generally even the longest and most horrific nondisclosure agreement will focus principally on these major items. If it's possible to say it simply, do yourself a favor and do so.

From signing of the confidentiality agreement it will typically take several more weeks to get the buyer the first phase of information, and for the buyer to consider their initial interest level. The faster buyers return to you with eager requests for further data, the better. Detailed questions are a good sign of real interest.

By the time you get to the stage of explicit response to buyer questions, you're likely to be at the three- or four-month mark. When you have a nice mix of interested parties, and you have provided them solid information, it is time to call for bids. Best buyers should, by this time, be fairly far along in their thinking, and able to establish price quickly. Bids can generally be requested with as little as a week's notice, if all is in place.

When bids are received, it is prudent to select more than one party to continue discussions with. Next phase actions will include invitations for tours of facilities, and meetings with the CEO or owner. Arranging such visits will probably take several more weeks, but, if all goes well, you will then be set to enter into a Letter of Intent with your chosen favorite, or move directly toward Definitive Purchase Agreement.

It shouldn't take more than a few weeks to negotiate the formal Definitive Agreement, and not more than another 60–90 days to complete due diligence and close. Save all possible time by encouraging buyers to progress on due diligence, financing, and any other matters, even as you complete the negotiations. If there's a problem or a hitch, it's better for everyone to face it as soon as possible, and either resolve it or move on.

Regarding timing—keep in mind that faster is ALWAYS better. A hundred things can go wrong, and foil the sale. A handful of things always will go wrong—inevitably. They have to be fixed, and fixed, and fixed again to stay on track. The tighter the timeframe, the less opportunity for fate to introduce all new and not all fun challenges to your successful completion of sale.

Choosing the "Best" Buyer

As ANY SELLER contemplates alternatives in consideration if inbound offers, there will often be a complex blend of apples versus oranges, to complicate the task of choice. In over half of the transactions we close, the winning choice is often not simply the highest bidder.

Owners may bias that final decision to any number of other factors, such as:

(1) Their perception of likely post-sale success for the company and the people they leave behind

(2) Their assessment of likelihood for a "clean" and fast sale, without unduly burdensome post-close indemnifications or complications

(3) Attractiveness of a proposed post-sale employment role for the exiting owner, for the time he expects to work in transition

(4) Confidence in the commitment of the chosen buyer, to come through with a closing quickly and without changes to the proposed deal structure

These and more, even finer discrepancies among offers, are absolutely valid and prudent factors for selection.

Several years ago we sold a company, which manufactured an air freshener product, which was distributed in housewares stores, in pet stores, and in several of the large discount chain stores. The company was small, but was growing rapidly, and was extremely profitable. After a few months' effort, we had about fifteen offers for our client seller. Ten of those offers were in the $15 to $20 million price range. Three of those offers were between $20 and $30 million. Two offers were more—with one at $32 million, and one at $35 million.

Our seller client chose the $32 million offer. Why? He felt that this buyer **(a)** *would treat his people well, and nurture the company's growth more effectively, and* **(b)** *that this buyer had a nicer, and more balanced group of negotiating staff, who he felt would be reasonable to work with, all the way to completion of the sale deal.*

The buyer's balance and finesse caused them to get the deal for about 10% less than another contender. Also, after all was said and done (now several years ago), our client remains pleased with his choice.

Sellers are right to trust their instincts in selection of buyers. In every case, there will be some transition time (for a minimum of a few months, up to perhaps even several years) when the exiting CEO will need to work with the new owners to facilitate the change. If the choice was poor, that can be a tough period of time. Also, because many "letter of intent" agreements between buyers and sellers either don't make it to close, or make it to close only after significant renegotiated terms and pricing, the choice of balanced and fair-minded buyers can increase the probability of close dramatically, and thus save sellers tremendous hard work and heartache in completing their transaction.

The best protection the seller can require, in order to ensure a sound selection, is to negotiate all possible big issues in ADVANCE of accepting an offer. As you discuss details of employment agreements, noncompetes, and seller warranties and indemnifications, you will quickly come to a fairly solid understanding of your new buyers' perspective.

After a handful of such discussions with your top few contenders, the best choice will often become fairly clear.

CHAPTER 4

Negotiating Techniques

The Value of Rapport

THERE IS A tremendous advantage to establishing a heartfelt and sincere like-each-other rapport with the other side to the transaction. Every element of the negotiation will proceed more smoothly with a pleasant relationship at the foundation. There are two great keys to establishing such a personal rapport.

The first is to make a sincere effort to get to know the other party, and to cause them to feel that they know you. When we know that someone has values similar to ours, family issues familiar to us, or other core commonalities, we naturally tend to feel that we understand them slightly better. We have a natural desire to please and get along with people that we understand, and people that we deem to be "friends."

Remember to be respectful and courteous toward the other person's personal religious, political, or ethnic views, even when they are vastly different from your own. *If you can't keep your mind open, keep your mouth shut too.*

My firm was once representing a buyer in the search for a specific niche manufacturer. After exhaustive research, we found the perfect company, based in rural Arkansas, and owned by a staunchly religious Southern Baptist family. In getting acquainted with the perspective seller, we learned that (a) he didn't drink, gamble, smoke, dance, or play cards, (b) he lived in a dry county and was proud to tell us that most of the local employees were of similar conservative background, (c) he leaned to the extreme right politically, and (d) he felt that the character of the possible buyer might well be more important to him in sale than any other factor—including price. We communicated all of this very explicitly to our somewhat wild and wooly New York client, and after about forty hours of patient discussions with the seller, we were finally able to arrange a meeting. We flew and drove for a long trip to arrive at the seller's place of business late in the day. The buyer sent his son from their Los Angeles plant to represent him at the meeting. The son showed up in an "Elton John Aids Benefit" T-shirt, with long hair and a ponytail, carrying a huge Santa-style mesh bag of beer-logo cups as a gift for our seller friends. The deal was literally dead before we even got inside the door.

Although you don't need to share the other party's perspectives or philosophies, you do need to be sincerely respectful of their viewpoint, at minimum.

The second key to building personal rapport is laughter. It's amazingly hard to dislike someone whom you laugh with. It's also amazingly hard to get seriously tough in negotiations with such a third party.

*Legendary baseball great, Dizzy Dean, was once up to bat, and, reacting to a called strike, he shouted at the umpire, "You jerk, that ball was a mile high!" The ump scowled at Dizzy, shook his head, and said, "Come off it, Dizzy, that ball was coming so fast you didn't even see it." Dizzy understood the potential penalty of a hostile, angry ump calling those pitches for the rest of the game, and he thought fast. He shuffled his feet a little, kicked at the bat, and looked like a sulky kid, while he mumbled, "Well, it sure **sounded** high." The ump laughed, and couldn't help but like Dizzy just a little bit more for the rest of the game.*

Those who laugh with us naturally find it difficult to feel antagonistic or hostile toward us.

F. Lee Bailey, one of the most notorious and successful defense attorneys of all time, has a famous bit of wisdom, which he has often shared with younger attorneys. Mr. Bailey says, "Laughing jurors don't convict." He has proven it literally hundreds of times.

One pertinent example may be the O. J. Simpson case. F. Lee Bailey was the original senior attorney on that case. Is it a coincidence that Johnny Cochran dotted his defense strategy with little bursts of thinly disguised play? Was it pure personal whimsy to compose little rap-like ditties for his defense remarks? Probably not. "If it don't fit, you must acquit!" Jurors laughed. They couldn't help but find Cochran amusing in a warm and playful way. True to the traditional F. Lee Bailey advice, those jurors did not convict.

Playing Hard To Get

IN THE BUSINESS of selling businesses, we tease about the need to give remedial lessons to our male staff members in "playing hard to get." Such gamesmanship truly does have a place in the sophisticated world of mergers and acquisitions.

An eager buyer, who believes competitors will want the target company, will pay more. He will pay faster. He will be less squeamish about fine points and details of the negotiated terms that don't go his way. The last thing in the world that he wants is to give his competitor an opening to get a foot into the door of "his" deal, simply because he was a little too slow, or he tried a little too hard to get a bargain. He will even, if necessary, pay a premium price to prevent competitive intrusion.

Thus it pays to be sensitive to the details that cause buyers to feel the heat of competition. If you, as seller, call every few days to check on status of the deal, will that whet the buyer's appetite? Of course not! If you do that he will see that you are chasing.

Take a lesson from your adorable 16-year-old daughter. The phone rings. She glances at the caller ID, smiles and says, "Tell him I'm not home, please Dad." Dad hangs up the phone; she smiles, tosses her head, and says, "Thanks." This girl will never be the chaser, and the boys know it. It only makes them want her more.

Take a lesson from professional athletes. Look at what happened to their compensation with the advent of free agent status.

The seller who is pursued by multiple buyers is much different from the seller who must chase buyers. Buyers will view the two entirely differently. If the seller initiates each step in the chase, the buyer will assume that there aren't many alternative suitors out there. If there were others, surely this seller would not seem so desperate.

The prudent seller remains cool enough to let the buyer chase him. Answer questions, and be responsive, but do not chase.

Mirroring

ONE OF THE greatest people techniques in the world, with almost universal applicability, is something referred to by psychologists as "mirroring." Basically, "mirroring" involves matching another person's style or mood, in order to establish a better connection. It's a magnificent technique helpful in negotiating, in selling, and even in general human relationships—business or personal.

It works amazingly well! It's hard to appreciate how extraordinarily effective it is unless you try it. The simplest, fastest way to get acquainted with mirroring might be tried the next time you come home to a depressed or sad spouse or sweetheart. Often our natural tendency in that circumstance is to help them out of the mood with a smiling "cheer-up, honey-bun!" We smile brightly, and try to keep in place our sunniest possible disposition to pull them up.

Next time, try instead to go down and join them in their misery. Empathize with their woes, and chime in with your own as well. Wallow with them in abject despondency.

Within thirty minutes (sometimes within five), you'll find them starting to pick up. They clearly feel better. Is it because they wanted you sad also? Of course not! It's simply human nature to feel more connected with someone there, on our own wavelength. It is a fact of our basic humanity that such a connection with another person (especially someone we love and trust) makes us feel better. Pretty soon, you'll find them cheering you up with jokes and lighthearted suggestions for fun activities.

Great salesmen very often mirror altogether naturally, without ever a thought. If their prospect speaks with an accent, they take on a hint of similar accent of their own. If the prospect speaks softly, they do too. If he sprawls in his chair, they take on a like posture. Connection is enhanced.

Mirroring can feel unnatural at first, but if you practice it, with your focus on the other person instead of yourself, you'll find that it quickly becomes very easy. It helps not only how you're received, but also how effectively you listen. Make it a part of your interpersonal skill base and natural style. It will pay off in multiple ways, for everything from discussing house rules with your teenager, to winning the last million dollars in a multi-million dollar deal.

Years ago, in my Big 8 CPA firm days, I attended a new seminar every year for some sort of management or leadership style analysis and coaching. I learned what "type" of style I had under at least a half a dozen different nomenclatures. Whether it was a "Q-1" or "A B" or "11:00", or whatever that particular system "named" each style, the meaning of the labels typically focused upon people vs. task orientation, introversion vs. extraversion, and other various behavioral spectrums.

In the end, almost every one of these analysis systems sought to tell us how to better deal with others who operated under different styles—emphasizing especially those with different focus or priorities from our own. We learned that the aggressive speaker with enthusiastic gestures and direct style might have difficulty communicating with the quiet, reserved person. I, being the friendly, direct, and inordinately enthusiastic type, learned that for some people I needed to pipe down in order to be best appreciated. No gestures. Quiet voice. No intrusion into the other person's space. Fact-oriented discussions, with references to instinctive or emotional factors left out.

In one particularly difficult relationship of those days, with one superior, my relationship improved literally overnight when I began to communicate in his style. He was the quiet, reserved, and all-quantitative-fact type, so I adapted to his style. I was quiet, purely factual, and tidy and contained in my every communication with him. He commented about eight months after I started this focused attention to style, that I had improved in technical performance amazingly in a very short time. He said I had grown more technically in the last eight months than I had in the preceding eight years.

In reality, I'm sure I was no better technically. I simply had finally learned how to talk with him in a way that was comfortable enough for him to hear. That was the year I made partner with my big eight CPA firm, and his support may well have put me over the top.

Strategic Anger

IN THE COURSE of negotiations it almost never pays to openly demonstrate anger. I actually have become so accustomed to controlling and monitoring anger, that I found myself automatically turning on the calm recently when I was abruptly cut off in traffic by an overly anxious driver slipping on through a stoplight after it was red. The anger automatically caused me to mask, and to think quickly. I smiled and waved. His grouchy face turned immediately to a confused smile, as he waved back. I'm sure he wondered who that friend or neighbor was that he had cut off in traffic. It completely changed a most irritating moment to absolute fun.

Generally the objective is to remain calm and cool, even in the face of enormous adversity. However, sometimes, when those on the other side of the table cross over certain types of lines, a brief but intense show of hostility is warranted—and, yes, even required.

The moment to show the flair of anger may be:

(1) When needed as a protective device, to shield others, or

(2) When the opponent has wantonly failed to show a sense of quid pro quo for a qualified concession you granted.

Anger can be appropriate as the last-ditch protective or defensive device. If one party to the transaction has been unduly attacked or criticized by the opponent, and the person attacked is essential to happy settlement of the deal, it may be time to set down a foot, loudly. The victim of the attack can't be the one to draw the line in the sand. Anything he says or does in response to the attack will look weak.

At the same time, the attacker must be made to very clearly understand that he has stepped into dangerous territory. Sometimes intensely angry reactions, by anyone *except* the subject of the attack, can do a far better job of putting the attacker in his place.

> *At the tail end of an important negotiation several years ago, our client and I had chosen what we felt was a "best" offer among many. We had agreed to a sit-down-and-work-through-the-issues meeting, to try to come to resolution on the remaining points. During the course of the discussion the buyer made a highly insulting remark, impugning the character of my client. I "felt" my client's face darken in rage. I saved him from the outburst by first having the outburst, in full and flaming glory, myself. I said, in effect, "How dare you!" with rage and passion. I tiraded on for several moments in magnificent fury. The buyers blanched, and became tight-lipped and sullen at my accusations.*

At the end was an awkward silence. My client finally broke the silence with, "I'm hungry. How about a lunch break?"

Everyone in the room (except me—remaining dutifully angry) laughed with relief. At lunch my client told me that he was just about to tell the buyer to jump in a lake. (His words were more colorful—I'm being civilized for polite publication). He said he appreciated my defense, and that he probably couldn't have gotten past this, without those things having been said. Now he felt better able to listen calmly, and evaluate their actions in the next phase of discussions far more rationally and comfortably.

The buyer opened the meeting after lunch with an immediate and frank apology. He said he understood that all of our actions to date had been entirely in good faith, and that the tensions of the day had simply overcome his rational perception for a moment. My client accepted his apology with calm goodwill and grace, and the discussions proceeded. The entire remainder of the negotiations came off without a hitch—with impressive even-temperedness and reasonableness on both sides of the table.

The second circumstance I mentioned at the outset of this section involved unexpected reneging by the opposing negotiators on an issue where a clearly implied quid pro quo was in order. Successful negotiations require some balancing sense of give and take on both sides. If a stated concession, or even a strongly implied concession, is withdrawn after your acquiescence has been confirmed, the balance becomes off-center. The disingenuous party must be challenged. Resistance is in order. Bully tactics cannot be permitted. They will inevitably multiply. Undeserved acquiescence screams weakness. The buyer will know that there are more weak retreats where that one came from.

Instead of mildly accepting, the seller must step forward bluntly, and, with a measured bit of anger, say, "I'm sorry, but that really doesn't work for me."

All of this said, be forewarned that as negotiations for sale of a business continue for a prolonged time period, tension will increase, and it will become inevitably more tempting to react with anger. My mother told me, *"Everyone is entitled to stupid remarks sometimes. The problem is that some people abuse the privilege."* I find myself thinking of that bit of wisdom often in the final tense stages of any negotiation. Nevertheless, I squelch my anger, unless it's genuinely needed to make a point.

Think before you speak. "The trouble with talking too fast is that you may say something you haven't thought of yet.

Listening

SAGES THROUGH THE ages have known the power of great listening. *It has often been said that the best way to win an argument is with your ears, not with your mouth.*

With any negotiation, it is critical to get a real understanding of what the other side wants and values most in the deal. Obviously, the buyer wants to pay less and the seller wants him to pay more. However, there's so much more to the tapestry of a deal. Why does the buyer want the deal? What are the real triggers to his desire? Does he need additional sales volume? Does the geography have appeal? Is there a fervent desire to take this opportunity away from some competitor? Is the chief buyer's job at risk if he doesn't complete this acquisition? Understanding the core elements to the buyer's desire will allow the negotiator to know what pieces of the deal are likely to be non-negotiable, and what pieces may be more flexible. These elements also give the negotiator tips on how to heighten the buyer's desire throughout the process.

Great listeners hear the subtleties. One must have a firm grasp of subtleties to practice great dealsmanship.

When I was a youngster in the negotiating world, I heard the comment on more than one occasion that I had great peripheral vision. This compliment meant that I had a good eye for the small things. I had a tendency to notice the acute interest (or fear) in the eyes of the opposition on some little issue, which we may have assumed to be unimportant. I could also feel the forward momentum in the midst of the negotiation when we reached that magical point where we were close enough to satisfy the opposition. I had good instincts about how much was enough, which allowed me to make good judgments about when to stand firm and wait for the other side to acquiesce.

Most people can really only focus on one thing at a time. *Have you ever noticed that when you're driving, and looking carefully for an address, you turn down the volume on the radio?* You are adjusting to allow yourself full intensity of attention on what you're doing. When you're speaking during a negotiation, you're concentrating intensely upon what you have to say. However, to be a great negotiator you must simultaneously pay tremendous attention to how the listener is receiving your message. Also, when the other side speaks, shut up and listen with great intensity and with all antennae up.

Listening well offers additional advantages, even beyond what you hear. *A closed mouth gathers no foot.* When we're tense, and there's an overly long pause, it can be tempting to fill it. Rarely do pertinent or appropriate comments come from "filler." *Abraham Lincoln said, "Better to remain silent and thought a fool, than to speak out, and remove all doubt."* I like that.

Strong listening skills and acute peripheral vision can be a tremendous advantage in the negotiating arena, and are well worth careful cultivation for the aspiring negotiator. Listen and benefit.

Playback

We have all heard of empathetic listening techniques wherein you "playback," in your own words, what a speaker has just said to you. The object of this exercise is to confirm that you have heard and understood correctly. In a negotiating scenario, this can be a highly effective communication style.

First, it does the clear job of confirmation. If you play it back, but miss, your listener can hear what he has conveyed, and can correct any misconceptions.

In an intense negotiation, however, this technique actually does a great deal more psychologically.

My first meaningful exposure to the effective use of this technique was in negotiating for the purchase of a Division company for one of my clients. Our objective was to make the buy aggressively and directly, without allowing the seller to actively pit us against a range of competitive buyers.

As I spoke with the lead negotiator for the seller, I found him frequently using a playback technique to verify his understanding of the positions I had taken. This had a couple of interesting and somewhat difficult-to-handle impacts.

First of all, my emotional response to his generally very accurate recaps of our position was to feel that he was very fair-minded. He clearly was listening, and he seemed to be giving some level of fair recognition to my points, just by voicing them back. Accordingly, he seemed to be trying to understand my point of view. This made it hard to play rough with him. Somehow it felt inequitable or unfair not to reciprocate with honest appreciation of his position as well.

Secondly, the same style of fair-minded recap was selectively used to point out the magnitude of the things I was asking for. He said, "You think the company is worth X. We think it's worth Y.

You would like for us to commit to sale at X now, without further testing our position in the marketplace, by courting competitive bids. Is that right?"

Me, awkwardly: "Ah, ... yes."

Seller: "We would love to finish this transaction quickly and easily without a full blown shopping of the company to other buyers, but we really don't want to do that at X dollars. We need to either climb to a price where we feel confident that we're close to market, or postpone further discussions with your client until we've had time to at least probe the marketplace."

Drat. Nice save.

We raised our bid, and quickly closed the deal at a very handsome price to the seller. My buyer client made great use of the new business, and did well with the acquisition in spite of the high price, but I was frustrated by my inability to attain the company for him at a bargain purchase price.

In spite of the increase in pricing that the seller achieved, we did get the deal closed, which, in this case, was critical—almost regardless of price. Without the seller's calm, cool playback technique, I'm not sure we would ever have gotten to closure. For others in the transaction, like me, the disarming directness and sense of good will from that repeatedly fair playback of our position made a huge difference. It helped tremendously to make my client and me feel that we were being treated reasonably, in spite of tough pricing.

Avoid the Tells

In poker playing there is a phenomenon known by the pros as "watching for the tells." "Tells" are subtle little indicators of thought that typically include eye movements, facial expressions, or body postures consistently shown by a given player in a given situation. The player with the especially powerful hand may

*always lean back a bit, and guard visibility of his hand more care-
fully than normal. The player who draws a losing two or three
cards may hold unusually still, and concentrate on his cards very
intently, as if by studying his hand more carefully, he will prevent
himself from displaying his disappointment.*

IN NEGOTIATING A deal there are likewise very subtle signs of
acceptance or disappointment with proposed terms. Unlike the poker
player, the deal negotiator may not have the opportunity to see the
other side in action repeatedly. Accordingly, the reaction to the "tell"
must be much quicker, and based on an almost intuitive read of much
subtler signs.

*Several years ago, I was working with a client on a buy-side
project. My client wanted to make an offer on a manufacturing
company that was being marketed by that company's attorney.
The attorney was conducting a limited auction type of sale, and
would not give us a tip about his client's pricing expectations. I
knew that offers had already been submitted, and that we were
late in the process. My client felt that the business was probably
worth about $40 million for net stock. I was concerned that we
might be able to get by with a lower purchase price than the $40
million contemplated offer. My suggestion would have been to
start at $30 to $35 million. However, the client was worried about
missing the deal, and asked me to move forward with an offer at
the $40 million mark.*

*To make the offer, I set a face-to-face appointment with the
attorney, with the explanation that I would be in his city anyway,
and I simply preferred to discuss the matter in person. In reality,
my visit was not so casual. I felt that I needed to have the advantage of seeing his reaction to my proposal. The moment I
mentioned $40 million, I saw him glance down, and quickly mask
all expression. I knew instinctively from his reaction that we were
high. I immediately moved to correct my overzealous bid. I went*

on to explain that this price would be for gross assets only, and that the seller would, of course, have to pay back his approxi-mately $15 million in liabilities from the $40 million proceeds. This took our $40 million bid down to $25 million in one sentence.

I saw a quick mental calculation flash across his face, as he said "Okay ... I see." I could tell that we were still in the running. He then began to ask for clarification on other points of the deal, like employment contracts, noncompete agreements, etc. Quick change of topic in this manner is often a way to try to distance oneself from the point last mentioned (price, in this case). People tend to do this when they are worried about their reaction being too visible to the opposition. His desire to quickly move to the other details of our proposal reinforced my certainty about the adequacy of our price. Accordingly, I responded as hard line as possible on all of the remaining points.

The deal which I took back to my buyer client was $15 million less than he had originally been willing to pay, and with far supe-rior terms in a number of ways. The deal closed a fast 30 days later, and our client was delighted.

As a seller, remember: If at all possible, it is always prudent to avoid receiving a verbal presentation of the buyer's proposal. The written proposal gives you time to consider before responding, and avoids the risk of the opposition's analysis of your reaction. If a written presen-tation is impossible to arrange, and you're forced into a face-to-face meeting, be careful.

Try to be a little bit unpredictable in response in order to muddy the other side's ability to read your reaction. Vary the pace. React slowly on one point. Move in a quick, no—thought manner on the next. Pause—maybe even a little bit too long sometimes. Erratic timing makes it difficult to read the emotional content of your response. Choose your words carefully. Guard your posture and expressions, but don't freeze or be unnatural, and thus obvious in your control.

Generally, the more you can convey uncertainty, reluctance, or "close call, but probably not" in your response, the more the buyer is likely to solidify details in your favor. Be mysterious. *Put on your Mona Lisa face. (Yes—guys can have that, too!)*

The less the opposition can read into reactions about any element of the proposed terms, the better your negotiating position will be.

Meeting in the Middle

THERE'S A NATURAL inclination, when trying to reach a compromise solution, to "split it down the middle." Such a split has an automatic appearance or feeling of fairness.

If I, as a seller, want the noncompete agreement to run for one year, but you, as the buyer, have a five-year agreement in mind, it may well be fairly easy to get both of us to a three-year mid-point. If I ask for $12 million for my company and you offer $10 million, $11 million would "feel" like the fair compromise solution.

Accordingly, in the case where the mid-point value might be acceptable, or even desirable, this natural mid-point compromise mentality can be a very good thing. All too often, however, negotiators will find themselves in a situation where meeting at the halfway point is simply not an acceptable solution.

In those instances, I would suggest several things. First of all, this is probably not an advantageous moment to continue the discussion on the numerical issue at odds. Change the subject. Although some "You were there and I was here" mentality may very naturally be played back to you by the opposition later, you will have a far better chance of veering away from the split in the middle solution if you sidestep and steer away from the issue.

Consider the possibility of reshuffling the deck altogether, and changing the elements of bidding. If it's possible to take an extremely different tack, and actually change other key elements to the deal (such as what will be included in the sale), that may jolt things enough to make prior discussions about the numbers irrelevant. With luck, it may force you to start anew.

Alternatively, you might consider focusing upon other issues as if they were as important as, or even more important than the numeric starting point under discussion. That may give you the opportunity to re-approach the troublesome number later from a different tack. After you're well into the discussion of the diversionary point, it will be far easier to revisit your rationale for a completely different pricing mechanism.

For example, in the midst of a tense discussion about pricing of an offer, the seller might shift gears with an entirely new issue. "This employment contract is really a big issue for me. I've been told that I would probably have to commit to six months or a year transition. Your proposal, with a three-year employment requirement, simply puts us in another environment altogether."

As you chip away at other issues, and become more distant from the numeric point of contention, a clean re-approach becomes simpler and more likely to be feasible.

Sometimes however, it's impossible to avoid having the other side come back to you with a protest that you aren't being fair because you're not considering his even-handed "split" solution. As a last resort, there may be no way to avoid drawing a clear line in the sand. "I'm sorry, but this is one of those situations where a split down the middle just won't work. The bottom-line fact is that your offer simply isn't competitive at those numbers."

(Smack! Ouch!)

Of course, be as gentle, as sincere, and as straightforward as possible in delivering such news.

When meeting in the middle simply can't work, you must either, **(a)** find the creative solution, **(b)** force the other side to rise to the occasion or, **(c)** back away. It's one of the toughest tests of high end negotiating skills. *As Benjamin Franklin observed more than 200*

years ago, "One of the great secrets of life is in learning to make step-
ping stones out of stumbling blocks."

Good Cop/Bad Cop

THERE IS A technique known the world over, which is a classic in the negotiating arena. It's most often called something like "Good Cop/Bad Cop," in acknowledgment of the age-old police method of getting information. One negotiator is kind, reasonable and warm. His partner is mean-spirited and harsh in every way. The prisoner is nurtured toward a trusting relationship with the Good Cop. The trust is enhanced and built far more rapidly, by injection of the counter-force in the form of the notorious Bad Cop. Bad Cop attacks and belittles. Good Cop protects and sees reason. Prisoner becomes at ease with Good Cop, begins to feel indebted to Good Cop. He soon begins to confide and trust in Good Cop.

Teamwork is essential. It gives them someone else to shoot at.

One of the fascinating things about Good Cop/Bad Cop in a negotiating scenario is that it often can work quite effectively, even when all parties to the discussion know exactly what game is being played. The negotiator in the "prisoner" role has the opportunity to use the Good Cop sessions as a forum to vent. He can offer possible compromise solutions without losing face. He can threaten to cut off discussions without needing to go so far as to walk away. He can generally convey things more openly to the "good cop," without overtly committing to a fixed position. Prisoner: "I'm afraid if Bad Cop goes one step further on that issue, it will leave me with no choice but complete withdrawal."

The Good Cop simultaneously has the opportunity to put forth predictions of the likely results of the proposed actions. Good Cop: "I'll bet if you offered to personally guarantee the debt, Bad Cop would have to soften on his hard stance about insisting on all cash for this deal."

The entire interplay in the Good Cop/Bad Cop game is a mechanism for setting up fronts, communicating positions, and exploring alternatives. Bad Cop defines the hard line stance, while Good Cop is the sympathetic problem solver.

It's a wonderful game!

The Bluff

THERE ARE TIMES in the life of the negotiator when you will find yourself playing poker for big stakes with only a pair of deuces in hand. You may have no choice but to mask your fear, hold your chin high, and forge ahead.

Our firm was representing a national trade magazine in possible sale. The magazine was owned and published by a not-for-profit trade association that was in dire straits. The association was out of money, six months overdue on its rents for a very substantial space, and was besieged with criticism by its constituent members.

In surveying the trade association's holdings, we quickly determined that one of their assets of potential value was the national magazine publication. Although the magazine had consistently lost money for the association for ten-plus years, the revenue base was good, with premium advertisers at good margins. The verified subscriber count was focused and excellent, and it clearly looked like a venture, which, within an independent for-profit environment, could be strongly profitable.

As we explored possible suitors for the business, we quickly came to realize that there were only two "natural" suitors with likelihood of very strong interest. This publication catered to a niche market where there were clearly two dominant players competing for access to readers.

Very early in the process one of the two best suitors dropped out due to internal problems. We kept several other possible second tier contenders alive in the deal, to try to hold the feeling of competition. However, in reality we knew that we were down to one real contender.

When the bids came in, less than two months after we were originally hired, the one "best" buyer was more than five times higher than the next runner up.

We knew that this buyer would never have bid so heartily had they not feared the competition of the other big player in their niche. We did not tell them who the bidders were, or where they stood relatively. In order to solidify the feeling of competitive pressure, we insisted on maintaining our right to continue to discuss the sale with multiple suitors. In spite of the protests of our "best" buyer, we refused to enter into any form of "stop shop" (commitment to exclusivity) until agreement on the final definitive purchase document and completion of their due diligence.

Things proceeded along very rapidly, until about one week before we were scheduled to wrap up the transaction. At this last moment a problem was found regarding the association's title to a portion of its subscriber list.

The buyer said that this issue created a major problem for them, and changed their mind about their original pricing. Given this issue, they felt that they needed to lower their price by 20%.

Our instincts screamed that any concession in pricing at this late stage in the discussions would be a blatant acknowledgment of weakness. We feared that if we allowed such a precipitous drop in pricing, further drops would almost certainly follow.

We told the buyer that the deal was off. We said we would go back to the other bidders, rather than accept such a change.

We said that we were sorry, but that we did not believe other buyers would expect this issue to lower price to any significant extent. Accordingly, if they insisted on pressing this issue, we would simply have to abandon their proposal, and return to the other buyers.

Our client was shocked, dismayed, and panicked at our response. This offer was more than five times greater than the next runner up, and they did not want to lose it. We explained that we believed that the buyer would lose faith in the overall deal immediately if they realized that their competition was not in the hunt. Further, we believed that acceptance of such changes to the deal could well tip them off about the weakness of the competition, and thus foil their appetite entirely. We finally convinced our client to remain silent, calm, and firm for at least three days, while the buyer contemplated alternatives.

Thankfully, we didn't need three days, as it turned out. Six hours after our original "No" response, the buyer called us and said, "Never mind. We're back on at the original price." We closed the deal one week later, as originally scheduled for an all cash price that was magnificent.

CHAPTER 5

Conclusion

IF AFTER READING this book you find that you look forward to the day when you enjoy the security of personal wealth garnished from the company you have built, where do you go from here to ensure that end-game goal?

First of all, you are on the right path simply by beginning to learn about what creates value in your company, and how the path to that end-game goal works! The appendix to this book includes a value-building checklist to help you to plan the course. A quarterly or more frequent pulse check of the estimated value achieved to that date, is an excellent and healthy step in the right direction. As you begin to understand that value, and chart a course to watch it build, you solidify your position and greatly enhance your probability of "readiness" when your time comes.

One of my clients has a favorite saying. He likes to remind people that "the guy at the top of that mountain didn't fall there, and he didn't wander up the slope by accident." You can't hit a target that you aren't looking at. The "target," or the reward you get for building a powerful, valuable, and salable company, is the ultimate freedom of financial security for a lifetime. The satisfaction of transitioning that company that you've built to give it an even bigger, better, and more secure future for the precious people who run it going forward, is the ultimate good feeling! Even as those great people move on in later years to other jobs and other places in their lives, they will always thrive and benefit from what they learned and developed in the building process. (One of the companies which our firm sold almost ten years ago has now gone on to produce at least four entrepreneurial business leaders. Today all of them are worth more financially than the original founder's entire company was worth when we initially took on their engagement. The founder was a genius and a great leader whose efforts multiplied the lifetime value and productivity of the company for a whole crew of the young people around him who watched and learned. And that has happened over a mere ten-years' time!)

Prepare your people, and prepare your company to nurture and to harvest great value for the future. Remain alert to change, and to the opportunities for sale when the right suitors begin to admire what you have built. Hire strong, professional help when the time comes, both to nurture competition, and to protect yourself by requiring solid and well-defined terms to the deal you may strike.

The goal of making your company "ripe" for the future, is one of the most satisfying and rewarding goals you will pursue in your lifetime. May you harvest the great rewards that you have earned, and enjoy building your business to become RIPE.

Appendices

Glossary of Middle Market Merger & Aquisition Terms

AAA
American Arbitration Association

Acquisition Corporation
A separate corporate entity established for the purpose of being the holding company for a given acquisition or acquisitions (typically utilized to protect assets of the buying owners from legal action in the event of problems).

Affiliate
A secondary party related by virtue of commonality of ownership, family relationship, or other connections, which create common interests.

Arbitration
An agreed procedure for resolving disputes outside of formal legal proceedings (resulting arbitrator decisions may be binding or nonbinding, depending upon agreement of parties in advance).

Asset Purchase
The purchase of named assets (and potentially the assumption of named liabilities) of a company (as opposed to a stock purchase, where only outstanding stock ownership is transferred).

Bad Faith
Any action done with the intent to deceive or mislead.

Basket
A commonly used "reserve" devise to accumulate claims in an ongoing tally, for eventual payment or reimbursement if certain aggregate thresholds or criteria are met (may be either reimbursement of amounts beyond the threshold, or a trigger of first-dollar reimbursement if the thresholds are met).

Business Broker
An agent who facilitates purchase or sale, usually for a percentage of price to be paid upon successful closure.

Call Option
An option contract that gives the holder the right, but not the obligation, to buy a certain quantity of an underlying security from the writer of the option, at a specified price, up to a specified date.

Closing
The finalizing of the sale of a company in which the ownership is transferred from the seller to the buyer.

Collar
Combinations of put options and call options that can limit, within a specific range, the risk that investment shares will drop in value (also generally limits potential for increased value).

Collateral Position
A security interest in specific named assets.

Confidentiality Agreement
A written agreement providing for secrecy between parties, and prohibiting use of confidential information by third parties. Also, often provides for restriction of use beyond a specific named purpose (such as evaluation of potential purchase).

Contingent Liabilities
Possible future liabilities, which may result in costs or damages if certain events occur.

Contingent Payment
A future payment which will only be required if certain conditions are satisfied.

Conversion Privilege
The right to convert one contractual right or privilege to another (for example, preferred stock which may be convertible to notes payable, or to common stock).

Cross Guarantee
Guarantees by multiple parties to secure the same indebtedness.

Deed of Trust
A document used in some states instead of a mortgage. Title is held by a trustee until the debt is satisfied and the deed of trust is released.

Definitive Agreement
The final governing agreement stipulating all detailed terms of an acquisition (also called the "Definitive Purchase Agreement").

Diminimus Rule
A provision for ignoring a certain contract privilege or obligation if the financial impact is less than some stated threshold level.

Due Diligence
The process of investigation, performed by the perspective buyers, into the details of a potential investment, such as the examination of financial data, operations and management, and the verification of material facts.

Earnings Multiple
A mechanism for business valuation which takes some measure of earnings (commonly either net earnings, earnings before interest and taxes, or earnings before interest, taxes, depreciation and amortization) and applies a "multiplier" to those earnings to arrive at enterprise value.

Earnout
A special additional benefit provision for supplemental payments to seller post-closing, to be paid only if certain specific financial or operating targets are met.

EBIT
Earnings before interest and taxes.

EBITDA
Earnings before interest, taxes, depreciation, and amortization.

EBT
Earnings before taxes.

Enterprise Value
A measure of the market value of a company's ongoing operations.

Equity Fund
An investment fund established for the purpose of buying equity interests in companies.

Escrow Agreement
An agreement which governs the use and distribution of funds or securities held or set aside pending resolution of certain specified matters.

ESOP
Employee Stock Ownership Plan—a tax-deferred retirement-benefit plan for employee ownership of a company—subject to ERISA regulations.

Exclusivity Agreement
An agreement whereby a seller promises to limit discussions or negotiations with only a single buyer, forsaking all others.

Extraordinary Item
An unusual and non-recurring event, which materially affected a company's finances in a reporting period.

Financial Buyer
A buyer who purchases companies, usually for stand-alone operation, to produce return on investment for its shareholders (generally not a "strategic buyer").

Financing Contingency
A provision, which makes the obligation for completion contingent upon ability to get borrowed funds.

Finder
An intermediary who generally provides limited services of finding a buyer or seller in an acquisition transaction.

First Collateral Position
The dominant security interest when multiple financing parties are providing funding for the same transaction, or for purchase of similar or related assets.

For Cause
Done in response to a specific incident or incidents. (for example, termination was "for cause" because the terminated employee committed theft or fraud).

Grandfather Provision
Allowable continuance of a practice that is now forbidden.

Gross Price
The total price a buyer pays for a company before expenses, commission, or other costs.

Hedge
To take an action in order to reduce the risk of adverse price movements in an asset. (A hedge on public stock received in sale might limit the seller's risk of accepting stock versus cash.)

Holdback
A contractual condition in which payment is withheld until a specific event occurs.

Horizontal Acquisition
Purchase of a company, which is either a direct competitor, or which, by its nature, could supply similar goods or services to some segment of the market-place.

Indemnification
A promise to protect a counterparty from damages resulting from misrepresentations or from certain named actions or conditions.

Intermediary
A third party who facilitates a transaction between two parties.

IPO
Initial public offering, the first sale of stock by a company to the general public or to investors.

Knowledge Qualifier
A provision which restricts a specific contractual warranty to be effective only if the representing party actually had knowledge of the matter at hand.

Letter of Intent
A preliminary agreement of good faith intent to move toward consummation of a buy/sell transaction.

Letter of Interest
A preliminary expression of expected value and possible purchase terms for a potential acquisition; also referred to occasionally as "expression of interest".

Lien
A legal claim against an asset, which is used to secure a loan or a lease.

Market Value Adjustment
An adjustment to current estimated market values, encompassing changes in the market climate or business fluctuations.

Material Information
Information, which is highly significant to value or to some other business judgment.

Mezzanine Financing
Late-stage financing (such as bids, warrants, preferred stock, or other) with both debt-like and equity-like characteristics; generally more expensive and more risky than senior debt, but less costly and less risky than equity capital.

Mirroring
Mimicking the communication style of another person in order to establish greater rapport.

Misrepresentation
Intentional concealment or distortion of information in order to deceive or mislead.

Nondisclosure Agreement
A written agreement providing for secrecy between parties, and prohibiting use of confidential information by third parties; often provides for restriction of use beyond a specific named purpose (such as evaluation of potential purchase).

No-shop
An agreement whereby a seller promises to continue discussions or negotiations exclusively with one buyer.

Note
A written agreement to repay debt.

Option
The right, but not the obligation to buy (call option) or sell (put option).

Personal Guarantee
A promise made by a guarantor which obligates him/her to personally repay specifically guaranteed debts in the event of default.

Phase I
The first level environmental review, typically involving site inspection, inquiries about practices and procedures, and review of governmental (EPA, sewer authority, etc.) and other records of historic environmental issues.

Phase II
The second level environmental review, usually initiated when there is a concern about a particular possible problem, and usually involving some specific site testing (soil samples, water testing, etc.).

Post-Closing Adjustment
A price adjustment made after closing, usually pursuant to specific terms set forth in the Definitive Purchase Agreement.

Post-Closing Audit
An audit performed after the closing, usually a financial audit done as of the closing date.

Preclosing
Events prior to the final closing date; may refer to a meeting shortly before a scheduled closing, the purpose of which is to walk through all documentation and make sure all is in order for a scheduled closing (i.e. a preclosing may be scheduled one day ahead of the closing date).

Present Value
The current value of future cash payments, discounted at an appropriate interest or "discount" rate.

Proceeds
Money received through a specific financial event, such as a sale or loan.

Put Option
An option contract that gives the holder the right, but not the obligation, to sell a certain quantity of an underlying security at a specified price up to a specified date.

Representation
A statement promising truth or fullness of disclosure with respect to a named matter.

Second Deed of Trust
A specific collateral interest, secondary to a primary secured party's first claim.

Secrecy Agreement
A written agreement providing for secrecy between parties.

Security Interest
The legal interest of a creditor in assets or real property perfected through the filings under the uniform commercial code and/or through the filing of a mortgage which establishes the creditor's right to the assets or property in the event of default on behalf of the debtor.

Senior Lender
Lender with the first collateral position on assets (usually a traditional bank, and usually the largest secured lender).

Shell Corporation
A corporate entity usually with little or no net worth and with no specific operating activities.

Stand Still Agreement

An agreement sometimes required by a lender, which limits the rights of others to foreclose on any security interests they may have in the same assets; also a term used loosely to refer to an exclusivity agreement (the seller will "stand still," and cease talks with alternative buyers).

Stop-shop

An agreement whereby a seller promises to continue discussions or negotiations exclusively with one buyer.

Strategic Buyer

A buyer which is an operating company in a related area of business, usually with interest in a given acquisition due to some type of likely synergy from the business combination.

Surviving Contract Provision

A contract provision, which will continue to remain effective after the rest of the contract has expired.

Triple Net Lease

A lease wherein the lessee is solely responsible for all of the costs relating to the asset being leased (taxes, insurance, maintenance, etc.).

Valuation Reserve

An allowance or contra-asset, established to provide for an anticipated diminishment in value of an asset (such as a reserve on inventories, to provide an allowance for unsaleable or obsolete items).

Vertical Acquisition

Purchase of a company, which is, or which, by its nature, could be a supplier to or customer of the buyer (said to be a "downstream" or an "upstream"; acquisition, respectively).

Warranty

A statement guaranteeing the validity of a certain assertion or representation.

Note: *The above definitions are intended to provide a general business understanding of the terms as most commonly used in middle market merger and acquisition discussions. Specific legal implications may differ depending on context, so always consult with legal advisors, and be attentive to contract-specific definitions within any agreement.*

APPENDIX II

Sample Nondisclosure

The undersigned hereby agrees:

That all information, data and materials disclosed or furnished (herein called the Information) relating to Douglas Group (hereinafter Douglas) client ABC (herein called the Company) will be maintained strictly confidential and that, in consideration for such disclosure, no use of the Information will be made by any signing party, or employees of such party, other than for internal evaluation purposes, on a strictly confidential basis.

It is understood that disclosure of any of the Information, including the possibility that the Shareholders may consider sale, disclosure of the current status of the Company, or disclosure of any information to customers, vendors, competitors, or employees of the Company would cause serious financial damage to the Company and/or its affiliates.

Further, the undersigned agrees not to copy, duplicate, disclose or deliver all or any portion of the Information to a third party or permit any third party to inspect, copy or duplicate the same. Additionally, the undersigned understands and agrees that all inquiries regarding the Company shall be made through Douglas, and no contact shall be made directly to the Company offices.

This shall not, however, prevent the undersigned from disclosing to others or using in any manner:

(1) Information which has been published and has become part of the public domain other than by acts or omissions by the receiving party.

(2) Information which has been furnished or made known to the undersigned by third parties as a matter of right without restriction of disclosure, or

(3) Information, which the undersigned can show was already in its possession at the time, it entered into this Agreement and which was not acquired directly or indirectly from the Company, their representatives, its employees, or their representatives

This agreement shall remain in effect for a term of two years from the execution date hereof and upon request, the receiving party will promptly return all data and materials furnished by Douglas and destroy any internal analyses and/or work papers related to the evaluation of the Company.

Signature _____

Name (please print)_____

Title _____

Company _____

Address _____

City/State/Zip _____

Phone _____

Fax _____ **Email** _____

Date _____

APPENDIX III

Seller Information Checklist

GENERAL INFORMATION

Narrative Overview:
  Description of key aspects of business; Executive Summary

Financial Overview:
  Recap of key financial indicators
  Most recent 3–5 years, and often forward projections for a few years
  Sales, gross margins, EBIT, EBITDA, and key balance sheet data

FINANCIAL DATA

Pertinent Recast Financial Information:
  Owners' compensation
  Unusual or nonrecurring costs
  Family or personal discretionary expenses

Audited Financial Statements:
  Usually past 3–5 years

Internal Financial Statements:
  Usually most recent year to date and comparable year to date prior year

Gross Margin Analysis:
  History of margins by major product or service segment

MARKETS

Brochures

Market Potential Overview:
Discussion of major areas of growth potential

Sales by Market:
  History and trends by major market segment (including market share data)

Major Competitors:
Size, geography, and some strength/weakness analysis

Sales by Territory:
History and trends by geographic or territorial segmentation

Analysis of Sales Channels:
Systems utilized, use of inside staff, reps, etc.

Customer Dependency Analysis:
Often top 10 customer volumes without specific identification (to permit analysis of % dependency on largest few)

Backlog Reports:
Preferably comparable with past periods

Pending New Opportunities:
Description of significant proposals pending

FACILITIES & EQUIPMENT

Facilities Overview:
Description of major facilities by location

Real Estate Appraisals

Lease or Rental Recap

Equipment Listings

Equipment Appraisals

Technology/Systems/Computer Overview

Capital Expenditure Needs Analysis

PEOPLE

Organization Chart

Management Level Staffing:
Descriptions of backgrounds for top level managers

Staff Summary:
Description of employee titles, counts, and pay scales

Recap of Employee Benefit Plans

APPENDIX IV

Buyer Sourcing Checklist

GENERAL

General search for companies in right industry/right size (multiple accessible sources by SIC code)

Research of Merger and Acquisition paid databases

Equity fund buyers

General acquisition research of periodicals & newspapers (recent histories of major transactions)

Buyer intermediaries (valid source, but exercise caution—many send out mass mailings with thinly veiled description)

INDUSTRY SPECIFIC

Officers and executives of trade associations*

Editors and reporters of trade magazines*

Industry expert professionals (CPA's, attorneys, and consultants who specialize in the industry)*

Top company lists provided by business journals and trade periodicals

COMPANY SPECIFIC

Competitors

Major equipment suppliers*

Raw material suppliers*

Suppliers of adjacent goods or services to same customer base

Excellent sources of information, but require hands-on individual contact and conversation to gain meaningful data

APPENDIX V

Definitive Agreement Checklist

Purchase Price

Cash

Form of other consideration
> *If in part note, specify security or collateral*

Definition of what is being purchased
> *Identify any assets or liabilities to be excluded*
> *If real estate entity assets are to be included, detail terms*

Releases from seller personal guarantees
> *Specify that releases must be obtained to close*

Other agreements required for transaction (i.e. consulting, employment, noncompetes, collateral)
> *Specify details for any highly sensitive matters*

Deferred Purchase Payments

Amounts

Collateral

Guarantees

Definition of contingencies

Timing of payments
> *Consider definition of recourse for non-payment or non-compliance*

> *Provide clear rights for access to information on company, before payments are completed*

> *If deferred payments depend on company performance, restrict changes to staff, and restrict management fees to be levied*

Deposit

Amount required
Forfeiture privileges
Escrow requirements
Stop-shop

Timing

Closing date
Access to information during interim
Back-out privileges
Consider interim dates for completion of key items, or freedom from stop-shop if schedule lags

Representation and Warranties

Seller:
Clear title
Honesty and material accuracy (include critical info as exhibits—financial statements, key contracts, etc.)
Normal conduct of business
Has informed buyer of important matters or contingencies (enumerate)
Buyer:
Guarantor Financial Statements presented to seller are accurate
Material adverse events: definition and consequences
Intermediary fees
Cooperative transfer of contracts
Indemnifications
Other transaction-specific matters
Arbitration or dispute resolution process

Employment/Consulting

Time required
Nature of work
Payment timing
Benefits (vacation, health care)

APPENDIX VI

Sample Stock Purchase Agreement

THIS STOCK PURCHASE AGREEMENT (the "*Agreement*") is made and entered into as of the ___ day of _____, 201X, by and among [Purchasing Entity] ("*Purchaser*"), John and Jane Doe (individually and collectively, "*Seller*"), and ABC Company, a Missouri corporation (the "*Company*").

R E C I T A L S:

Seller owns _____ shares of the $_____ par value common stock of the Company, constituting 100% of all issued and outstanding capital stock of the Company. [There are _____ shares issued and outstanding; _____ are held as treasury stock.]

The Company is engaged in the business of_____ (the "*Business*").

Seller desires to sell, and Purchaser desires to purchase, for the consideration and on the terms set forth in this Agreement, the entire (___ shares), 100% of the issued and outstanding shares (the "*Shares*") of capital stock of the Company currently owned by Seller.

Accordingly, for good and valuable consideration, the receipt and sufficiency of which is hereby acknowledged, the parties, intending to be legally bound, hereby agree as follows. Capitalized terms used herein shall have the definitions set forth throughout this Agreement.

SALE AND TRANSFER OF SHARES

Shares. At the Closing and in reliance upon the representations, warranties and agreements and subject to the conditions set forth in this Agreement, Seller shall sell, assign, transfer, convey and deliver to Purchaser, free and clear of all liens, claims, options, charges, security interests, pledges, mortgages or other encumbrances whatsoever (collectively "Liens"), and Purchaser shall purchase, the Shares from Seller.

Consideration. The aggregate consideration to be paid by Purchaser for the Shares (the "Purchase Price") shall be _____ ($_____), payable in readily available funds at Closing (defined below) subject to Purchase Price Adjustment after Closing as described below.

Determination of Purchase Price Adjustments.

Closing Statement. Promptly, but in any event within 45 days after the Closing, Purchaser shall furnish to Seller a statement (the "Closing Statement") setting forth the Net Working Capital of Company as of the close of business on the Closing Date ("Closing Net Working Capital").

For purposes hereof, "Net Working Capital" means the excess of current assets less current liabilities as historically determined by Company and presented on Company's financial statements. Subject to the foregoing, Net Working Capital will be calculated in a manner consistent with the calculation of Net Working Capital of Company as of _____ as set forth on Schedule _____.

Dispute Resolution. If Seller disagrees with any item on the Closing Statement, Seller shall notify Purchaser in writing of such disagreement within 30 business days after Seller's receipt thereof (such notice setting forth in reasonable detail the basis for such disagreement). Purchaser shall permit Seller access to such work papers relating to the preparation of the Closing Statement as may be reasonably necessary to permit Seller to review in detail the manner in which the Closing Statement was prepared. Purchaser and Seller shall thereafter negotiate in good faith to resolve any such disagreements; provided, however, that Purchaser shall within five (5) business days pay to Seller the amount determined pursuant to Section ____ below which is not subject to dispute, if any. If Purchaser and Seller are unable to resolve any such disagreements within 30 days, Purchaser and Seller shall jointly retain an [Independent Accounting Firm] (the "Auditor"), who has not provided any services to Purchaser or Seller during the twenty-four month period preceding the date of this Agreement, to resolve any remaining disagreements in accordance with the terms of this Section ____. Purchaser and Seller shall direct the Auditor to render a determination within 25 days of its retention and Purchaser and Seller shall use their reasonable best efforts to cause the Auditor to resolve all disagreements over individual line items as soon as possible. The Auditor shall consider only those items and amounts in the Closing Statement which Purchaser and Seller are unable to resolve. The determination of the Auditor shall be conclusive and binding upon Purchaser and Seller. The fees and expenses of the Auditor shall be allocated to be paid 50% by Purchaser and 50% by Seller.

Net Working Capital Adjustment. If Closing Net Working Capital exceeds $_____,[1] Purchaser shall pay to Seller an amount equal to the excess. If Closing Net Working Capital is less than $_____, then Seller shall pay to Purchaser an amount equal to the deficiency.

Adjustment Amount. Without duplication, all amounts owed pursuant to Section ____ shall be aggregated, and the net amount (if any) owed by Purchaser to Seller, on the one hand, or Seller to Purchaser, on the other hand, is referred to as the "Final Adjustment Amount". The Final Adjustment Amount shall be calculated as an adjustment to the Closing Purchase Price on the first business day on which the Closing Statement becomes conclusive and binding. Payment of the Final Adjustment Amount shall be paid by delivery of immediately available funds to an account designated by the recipient party within five (5) business days after the date of final determination.

CLOSING

The Closing. Subject to Article ____, the closing of the transactions contemplated hereby (the "Closing") shall take place on _____*(date)* (the "Closing Date"), at the offices of the Company or at such other time or place as the parties hereto shall agree to in writing.

Seller's Deliveries. Subject to the conditions set forth in this Agreement, at the Closing, simultaneous with Purchaser's deliveries hereunder, Seller shall execute and deliver or cause to be executed and

---

[1] The Net Working Capital of _____as of _____.

delivered to Purchaser all of the following documents and instruments, all in form and substance reasonably satisfactory to Purchaser and its counsel;

Resignation. Seller's resignation as an officer and director of the Company, as well as trustee under any 401(k), profit-sharing, pension or similar retirement plan of the Company, effective as of the Closing Date (provided, Seller may be elected as an officer on or shortly after Closing);

Required Consents. The Required Consents (as defined in Section _____), if any, which Purchaser shall cooperate with Seller in obtaining;

Organizational Documents. The original Articles of Incorporation and bylaws of the Company and all amendments, if any, and the original minute books, stock records and stock ledgers of the Company;

The Shares. Stock certificates representing the Shares, duly endorsed (or accompanied by duly executed stock powers) for transfer to Purchaser;

Additional Agreements. All such other documents and instruments as Purchaser or its counsel shall reasonably request in connection with the consummation of the transactions contemplated by this Agreement;

Purchaser's Deliveries. Subject to the conditions set forth in this Agreement, at the Closing, simultaneous with the deliveries of Seller hereunder, Purchaser shall execute and deliver or cause to be executed and delivered all of the following documents and instruments, all in form and substance reasonably satisfactory to Seller and their counsel;

Closing Payment. The Purchase Price as provided in Section 1.2 hereof;

REPRESENTATIONS AND WARRANTIES OF SELLER

Seller hereby represents, warrants and covenants to Purchaser as follows:

Organization and Authority. The Company is a Missouri corporation duly organized, validly existing and in good standing under the laws of the State of Missouri and has all requisite power and authority (corporate and other) to own, lease and operate its properties and assets and to conduct its business as now being conducted.

Capitalization. The authorized equity securities of the Company consist of _____ shares of common stock, $_____ par value per share, of which _____ shares are issued and outstanding. At the Closing, all of Seller's right, title and interest in the Shares will be transferred to Purchaser, free and clear of all Liens. No legend or other reference to any purported Lien appears upon any certificate representing equity securities of the Company. All of the Shares of the Company have been duly authorized, validly issued and are fully paid and non-assessable. Company has not granted any option or right to purchase or convert any obligation into shares of the capital stock of the Company, issued any security convertible into such capital stock, granted any registration rights or purchased, redeemed, retired or otherwise acquired any shares of such capital stock. None of the Shares of the Company was issued in violation of any Rule (defined below), including any applicable federal or state securities laws. The Company does not own any subsidiary.

Authority Relative to Agreement. Seller has the power and authority to enter into this Agreement and any agreement, instrument or document executed and/or delivered by the Seller in connection herewith or contemplated hereby (all such additional agreements, instruments and documents executed or delivered by any party in connection with this Agreement being called the "*Additional Documents*") and to carry out Seller's obligations hereunder and thereunder. This Agreement and the Additional Documents have been duly executed by the Seller and are the valid and legally binding obligations of Seller, enforceable against Seller in accordance with their terms.

Absence of Conflicts. The execution, delivery and performance by the Seller of this Agreement and the Additional Documents, and the transactions contemplated hereby and thereby, do not and will not conflict with or result in any violation of or constitute a breach or default under any term of any agreement, permit or other instrument to which the Seller or the Company is a party, or by which the Seller is bound or to which any of the Company Assets or the Business is subject, or any order, judgment or decree of any court or other Governmental Authority to which the Seller, the Company Assets or the Business is bound or subject, or any law, statute or regulation of any Governmental Authority, and will not result in the creation of any Lien upon any of the Company assets.

Books and Records. All of the books and records, contracts, vendor files, vendor lists and records, cost files and records, credit information, distribution records, business records and plans, Tax returns and other Tax records, studies, surveys, reports, correspondence, sales and promotional literature and materials, computer and other records, all computer software, and all similar data, documents and items, wherever located (collectively, the "Books and Records") are to Seller's knowledge accurate and complete and have been maintained in the Company's usual, regular and ordinary manner, and all transactions of the Company are properly reflected therein.

Financial Statements. Purchaser has had access to copies of (a) the balance sheet of the Company as of the last day of each of the two fiscal years of the Company preceding the year of this Agreement, together with the related income and cash flow statements (the *"Fiscal Year Financial Statements"*), and (b) the internally prepared balance sheet of the Company as of _____ (the *"Balance Sheet Date"*), together with the related unaudited income statement (the *"Interim Financial Statements"* and, together with the Fiscal Year Financial Statements, the *"Financial Statements"*). Each of the Financial Statements (i) fairly and accurately presents the financial position and results of operations of the Company as of such date and for the period then ended, (ii) is accurate, correct and complete and in accordance with the books and records of the Company, and (iii) can be reconciled with the books and records, financial statements and the financial records maintained and the accounting methods applied by the Company for federal income tax purposes.

Absence of Certain Changes or Events. Other than the transactions outlined in the Purchaser's Letter of Intent dated _____ and presented in Schedule _____, there has not been any development (including, without limitation, consummation of the transactions contemplated hereby) or, to Seller's knowledge, threatened development (other than general economic conditions) of a nature which may cause any adverse change in the financial condition, net worth, assets, liabilities, personnel, prospects or operations (including, without limitation, the Company's relationship with suppliers, employees, clients and others) of the Business or the ability of the Seller to perform this Agreement and the Additional Documents (collectively, *"Adverse Effect"*).

Compliance with Laws. The Company is not in violation of, and the Business is being conducted in accordance with, all federal, state, municipal, foreign and other laws, regulations, orders and other legal requirements applicable thereto (collectively, *"Rules"*), the failure to comply with which could have an Adverse Effect, and Seller does not have knowledge of, nor has the Company or the Seller received notice of, any violation or alleged violation by the Company of any Rule or that the Company is in default with respect to any order, judgment, award, injunction or decree of any court or Governmental Authority or arbitrator, applicable, in any such case, to the Company, the Business or any of the Company Assets.

Taxes. The Company has properly completed and filed on a timely basis and in correct form all tax returns relating to all excise, payroll, real estate, capital stock, intangible, value-added, income, sales, use, service, employment, property and, without limitation of the foregoing, all other taxes of every kind and nature which the Company has been required to file. No claim with respect to the Business has ever been made by an authority in a jurisdiction where the Company does not file Tax returns that the Company is or may be subject to taxation by that jurisdiction. All taxes of the type herein referred to (whether or not requiring the filing of returns), including all deficiency assessments, additions to tax, penalties and interest (collectively, *"Taxes"*), have been paid to the extent and to the extent not due or not paid but contested, have been properly accrued on the Company's books and records and segregated to the extent required by sound accounting practice. The Company or the Seller has not received any notice of and the Company or Seller does not have any knowledge or reason to know of any Tax deficiency proposed or threatened against Company.

Undisclosed Liabilities. To Seller's knowledge, the Company does not have any obligation or liability, absolute or contingent, known or unknown, liquidated or unliquidated, whether due or to become due and regardless of when or by whom asserted, not shown or provided for in the Financial Statements, except for liabilities which are immaterial (individually and in the aggregate) to the Business. As of the Closing Date, Company shall not have any obligation or liability, absolute or contingent, known or unknown, not shown or provided for in the Interim Financial Statements.

Contracts. Purchaser has had access to each contract, agreement or commitment of whatever nature or description, whether oral or written including, without limitation, related to the Business (the *"Contracts"*) to which the Company is a party or by which it or any of its property is bound, other than those listed on Schedule ____. To Seller's knowledge, The Company has performed all obligations required to be performed by it under all Contracts. To Seller's knowledge, Company is not in default under any of such Contracts or has waived any of its rights under any of such Contracts, and each Contract is in full force and effect as of the date hereof.

Litigation. The Company or Seller does not have any actions, suits, proceedings or investigations, or any claims, actions, suits, proceedings, labor disputes or investigations pending or, to the best of Seller's knowledge, threatened before any court or Governmental Authority, or before any arbitrator of any nature, brought by or against the Company, or any of its directors, officers, stockholders, employees or agents involving, affecting or relating to any of the Business, any Company assets or the transactions contemplated by this Agreement or the Additional Documents, nor, to the best of Seller's knowledge, is there any basis for any such action, suit, proceeding or investigation. The Company, the Business or any Company Asset is not subject to any order, writ, judgment, award, injunction or decree of any court or Governmental Authority or arbitrator, which affects or which might affect the Company, any of the Company Assets or the Business, or which would or might interfere with the transactions contemplated by this Agreement or the Additional Documents.

Consents. No notice to, and no permit, authorization, consent or approval of, any federal, state, local, foreign or other governmental or regulatory authority (*"Governmental Authority"*) or other **third party is** necessary for the consummation by the Seller and the Company of the transactions contemplated by this Agreement or the Additional Documents.

EMPLOYEE PLANS.

Identification. All Company bonus, pension, stock option, stock purchase, benefit, welfare, profit sharing, retirement, disability, vacation, severance, hospitalization, insurance, incentive, deferred compensation, 401(k) or other similar fringe or employee benefit plans, or any employment contracts or executive compensation agreements, written or oral, in each of the foregoing cases which cover, are maintained for the benefit of, or relate to any or all employees of the Company (collectively the *"Employee Plans"*) are set forth on Schedule _____. Purchaser has had access to all manuals, brochures or publications or similar documents of the Company regarding office administration, personnel matters and hiring, evaluation, supervision, training, termination and promotion of employees of the Company, (collectively the *"Personnel Documents"*).

Documentation. With respect to the Employee Plans and Personnel Documents, Seller has made available to Purchaser true and complete copies of all prior plans, documents and related documents.

Code and ERISA. All Employee Plans are, and at all times were, in compliance, in form and operation, with the requirements provided by any and all statutes, orders or governmental rules or regulations then or currently in effect. All required reports and descriptions of any Employee Plans have been timely filed and distributed.

Contributions, Accrual and Termination. With respect to any Employee Plans, all applicable contributions for all periods ending prior to Closing have been made in full. All insurance premiums have been paid in full with regard to such Employee Plan for policy years or other applicable policy periods ending on or before Closing. None of the Employee Plans has unfunded benefit liabilities. No accumulated funding deficiency has been incurred with respect to any Employee Plan, whether or not waived.

Withdrawal Liability. None of the Employee Plans is a multiemployer plan (a *"Multiemployer Plan"*).

Accuracy of Information. None of the representations, warranties or statements contained in this Agreement, in the Schedules or Exhibits hereto, or in any of the Additional Documents contains any untrue statement of a material fact or omits to state any material fact required to be stated therein or necessary in order to make any of such representations, warranties or statements, in the context in which made, not false or misleading. All documents (or copies thereof) referred to in the Schedules or Exhibits hereto have been delivered to Purchaser. All facts set forth in the Recitals are true and correct.

These representations and warranties shall survive for a period of one year form the closing date.

REPRESENTATIONS AND WARRANTIES OF PURCHASER.

Purchaser hereby represents, warrants and covenants to Seller as follows:

Authority. Purchaser has the power and authority to enter into this Agreement and the Additional Documents and to carry out his obligations hereunder and thereunder. This Agreement and the Additional Documents will be duly executed by Purchaser and will be the valid and legally binding obligations of Purchaser, enforceable against Purchaser in accordance with their terms.

Absence of Conflicts. The execution, delivery and performance by the Purchaser of this Agreement and the Additional Documents, and the transactions contemplated hereby and thereby, do not and will not conflict with or result in any violation of or constitute a breach or default under any term of any agreement, permit or other instrument to which the Purchaser is a party, or by which the Purchaser is bound, or any order, judgment or decree of any court or other Governmental Authority to which the Purchaser is bound or subject, or any law, statute or regulation of any Governmental Authority.

Investment Intent. Purchaser is acquiring the Shares for Purchaser's own account and not with a view to distribution within the meaning of the Securities Act of 1933, as amended.

These representations and warranties shall survive for a period of one year from the closing date.

COVENANTS.

Consents and Approvals. Seller shall obtain all necessary permits, consents, waivers, approvals, orders and authorizations of all Governmental Authorities and other persons or entities required to be obtained by such party hereto in connection with the execution, delivery and performance of this Agreement, the Additional Documents and the consummation of the transactions contemplated hereby or thereby by such party (the *"Required Consents"*).

Taxes. Purchaser shall have the right to review and approve the Tax returns for the Company for the period ending on or as of the Closing Date.

Investment Banking Fee. The Seller shall pay all fees due to _____ arising from this Agreement and the transaction contemplated hereby. All fees due _____ are to be paid at closing. Seller and Purchaser each represent and warrant to the other that they have not engaged any broker in connection with this Agreement other than _____.

RESTRICTIVE COVENANTS.

Proprietary Information. From and after the Closing Date, unless otherwise required by a court of competent jurisdiction, the Seller shall not, at any time, disclose to any individual, partnership, limited partnership, joint venture, syndicate, sole proprietorship, company or corporation with or without share capital, unincorporated association, trust, trustee, executor, administrator or other legal personal representative, regulatory body or agency, government or governmental agency, authority or entity (collectively, *"Person"*) or use for Seller's own benefit or for the benefit of any Person any confidential information (including, but not limited to, financial statements, methods by which the Business is or has been conducted, and methods by which the customers or business of the Company are or have been obtained) (collectively, the *"Proprietary Information"*) which does not exist in the public domain. The Seller shall deliver to the Purchaser at the time of execution of this Agreement all documents, memoranda, notes, lists, records, reports, and other documentation, whether embodied in a disk or in other form (and all copies of all of the foregoing), relating to the Business and any other Proprietary Information that the Seller may then possess or have under Seller's control.

Non-Competition. For a period of twelve (12) months after the Closing Date, the Seller shall not, directly or indirectly, engage or invest in, own, manage, operate, finance, control, or participate in the ownership, management, operation, financing, or control of, be associated or in any manner connected with, lend the Seller's credit to or render services or advice to, any business or Person whose products or activities compete in whole or in part with the products or activities of the Purchaser within a 200 mile radius of_____. The Seller agrees that this covenant is reasonable with respect to its duration, geographical area, and scope.

Non-Interference. For a period of twelve (12) months after the Closing Date, the Seller shall not, directly or indirectly, either for Seller or any other Person, (i) induce or attempt to induce any employee of the Purchaser to leave the employ of the Purchaser, (ii) in any way interfere with the relationship between the Purchaser and any employee of the Purchaser, (iii) employ, or otherwise engage as an employee, independent contractor, or otherwise, any employee of the Purchaser or (iv) induce or attempt to induce any customer, supplier, licensee, or business relation of the Purchaser to cease doing business with the Purchaser, or in any way interfere with the relationship between any customer, supplier, licensee, or business relation of the Purchaser.

Non-Solicitation. For a period of twelve (12) months after the Closing Date, the Seller shall not, directly or indirectly, either for Seller or any other Person, solicit the business of any Person known to the Seller to be a customer of the Purchaser, with respect to products or activities which compete in whole or in part with the products or activities of the Purchaser.

Acknowledgment. The Seller acknowledges and agrees that (i) the provisions of this Article above are reasonable and necessary to protect and preserve the Business; and (ii) the Purchaser could be irreparably damaged if the Seller were to breach the covenants set forth in this Article.

Remedies. The Purchaser will be entitled to obtain injunctive or other equitable relief to restrain any breach or threatened breach or otherwise to specifically enforce the provisions of this Article, it being agreed that money damages alone could be inadequate to compensate the Purchaser and could be an inadequate remedy for such breach.

INDEMNIFICATION.

Survival of Representations, Warranties and Covenants. The respective representations, warranties and covenants of each of the parties to this Agreement, including all statements contained in any Schedule delivered pursuant hereto, shall be deemed to be material and to have been relied upon by the parties hereto and shall survive the Closing and the consummation of the transactions contemplated hereby.

Seller's Indemnification. Seller shall indemnify and hold harmless Purchaser and the Company and its affiliates and their respective officers, directors, stockholders, agents, successors and assigns (collectively, *"Purchaser Indemnified Parties"*), from and against and in respect of any and all demands, claims, causes of action, administrative orders and notices, losses, costs, fines, liabilities, penalties, damages (direct or indirect) and expenses (including, without limitation, reasonable legal, paralegal, accounting and consultant fees and other expenses incurred in the investigation and defense of claims and actions) (hereinafter collectively called *"Losses"*) resulting from, in connection with or arising out of:

any incorrect or incomplete representation or warranty made by Seller in this Agreement or in any Additional Document delivered by Seller in connection herewith or therewith;

the failure of Seller to comply with, or the breach by Seller of, any of the covenants of this Agreement or any Additional Document;

any claim, action, suit or proceeding relating to any of the foregoing;

The conduct of the Business prior to Closing.

With respect to claims for breaches of representations and warranties referred to in Section ____ above, (i) Seller will be liable to the Purchaser for Losses arising there from only if the aggregate amount of all such Losses resulting to the Purchaser from all such breaches or claims exceeds _____ dollars ($____), and (ii) Seller shall not be liable to the Purchaser to the extent such Losses exceed _____ dollars ($_____). Any claims for indemnification under this agreement must be made within 12 months of the closing.

Purchaser's Indemnification. Purchaser shall indemnify and hold harmless Seller and his respective successors and assigns, from and against and in respect of any and all Losses resulting from, in connection with or arising out of:

any incorrect representation or warranty made by Purchaser in this Agreement or in any Additional Document delivered by Purchaser in connection herewith or therewith;

the failure of Purchaser to comply with, or the breach by Purchaser of, any of the covenants of this Agreement or any Additional Document; and

any claim, action, suit or proceeding relating to any of the foregoing.

With respect to claims for breaches of representations and warranties referred to in Section ____ above, (i) Purchaser will be liable to the Seller for Losses arising there from only if the aggregate amount of all such Losses resulting to the Seller from all such breaches or claims exceeds $_____, in which case Purchaser will be liable for all such Losses (including the initial $____); and (ii) Purchaser shall not be liable to the Seller to the extent such Losses exceed _____ dollars ($____). Any claims for indemnification under this agreement must be made within 12 months of the closing.

Cooperation. A party or parties against whom a claim for indemnification has been asserted (individually and collectively *"Indemnifying Party"*) shall have the right, at its own expense, to participate in the defense of any action or proceeding brought by a third party which resulted in said claim for indemnification, and if said right is exercised, the party or parties entitled to indemnification (individually and collectively *"Indemnified Party"*) and the Indemnifying Party shall cooperate in the defense of said action or proceeding.

CONDITIONS TO CLOSING.

Conditions to Obligations of Purchaser. All obligations of Purchaser under this Agreement are subject to the fulfillment, at or prior to the Closing, of the following conditions, any one or more of which may be waived by Purchaser:

Representations and Warranties of Seller. All representations and warranties made by Seller in this Agreement and in the Additional Documents shall be true and correct in all material respects on and as of the Closing Date and as of the time of the Closing, as if again made by Seller on and as of such dates.

Performance of Seller's Obligations. Seller shall have delivered all documents and agreements to which it is a party or signatory described in Section _____ and Seller shall have otherwise performed in all respects all obligations required under this Agreement and the Additional Documents to be performed by it or them on or prior to the Closing Date.

Consents and Approvals. The Required Consents shall have been duly obtained, unless waived in writing by Purchaser.

Pending Proceedings. No action or proceeding shall be pending before any court or Governmental Authority seeking to restrain or prohibit or obtain damages or other relief in connection with this Agreement or the consummation of the transactions contemplated hereby (including, without limitation, the Additional Documents) or the proposed operation of the Business by Purchaser.

No Adverse Change. During the period from the date hereof to the Closing, there shall have been no material adverse change which is expected to have an Adverse Effect.

Other Closing Documents. Purchaser shall have received such other certificates, instruments and documents, reasonably satisfactory in form and substance to Purchaser, in confirmation of the representations and warranties of each Seller or in furtherance of the transactions contemplated by this Agreement and the Additional Agreements as Purchaser or its counsel may reasonably request.

Financing. Purchaser shall have procured and closed on financing satisfactory to Purchaser to meet the Purchase Price requirements of Purchaser required by this Agreement.

Conditions to Obligations of Seller. All obligations of Seller under this Agreement are subject to the fulfillment, at or prior to the Closing, of the following conditions, any one or more of which may be waived by Seller:

Representations and Warranties of Purchaser. All representations and warranties made by Purchaser in this Agreement and the Additional Documents shall be true and correct in all material respects on and as of the Closing Date and as of the time of Closing, as if again made by Purchaser on and as of such dates.

Performance of Purchaser's Obligations. Purchaser shall have delivered all documents and agreements described in Section _____ and otherwise performed in all respects all obligations required under this Agreement and the Additional Documents to be performed by it on or prior to the Closing Date.

Other Closing Documents. Seller shall have received such other certificates, instruments and documents, reasonably satisfactory in form and substance to Seller, in confirmation of the representations and warranties of Purchaser or in furtherance of the transactions contemplated by this Agreement as Seller or their counsel may reasonably request.

MISCELLANEOUS PROVISIONS.

Successors and Assigns. This Agreement shall inure to the benefit of, and be binding upon, the parties hereto and their respective successors, heirs, representatives and assigns, as the case may be. Purchaser shall have the right to assign this Agreement to its owners or related parties. Nothing in this Agreement shall confer upon any person or entity not a party to this Agreement, or the legal representatives of such person or entity, any rights (including, without limitation, rights as a third party beneficiary) or remedies of any nature or kind whatsoever under or by reason of this Agreement.

Expenses. Each party to this Agreement will bear its respective expenses incurred in connection with the preparation, execution, and performance of this Agreement and the Related Agreements, including all fees and expenses of agents, representatives, counsel, and accountants.

Legal Fees. In the event a party hereto breaches this Agreement, the non-breaching party or parties shall be entitled to recover from the breaching party any and all damages, costs and expenses, including without limitation, reasonable attorneys' fees and court costs, incurred by the non-breaching party or parties as a result of the breach.

Notices. All notices, requests and other communications to any party hereunder shall be in writing (including telecopier or facsimile or similar writing), shall be given to such party at its address or facsimile number set forth below or at such other addresses as shall be furnished by any party by like notice to the others. Except as otherwise expressly provided herein, each such notice, request or other communication shall be effective upon the earlier of (i) actual receipt and (ii) receipt of confirmation of delivery, in each case at the address specified in this Section. Any notice, request or communication delivered by telecopier, facsimile or similar means shall be confirmed by hard copy delivered as soon as practicable.

if to Purchaser, to:

if to Seller, to:

if to Company, to:

or such other address or persons as the parties may from time to time designate in writing in the manner provided in this Section.

Entire Agreement. This Agreement, together with the Exhibits attached hereto, the Schedules and the Additional Documents, represent the entire agreement and understanding of the parties hereto with reference to the transactions contemplated herein and therein, and no representations, warranties or covenants have been made in connection with this Agreement other than those expressly set forth herein and therein. This Agreement supersedes all prior negotiations, discussions, correspondence, communications, understandings and agreements among the parties relating to the subject matter of this Agreement and all prior drafts thereof, all of which are merged into this Agreement or such other agreements, as the case may be.

Waivers, Amendments and Remedies. This Agreement may be amended, superseded, cancelled, renewed or extended, and the terms hereof may be waived and consents may be provided, only by a written instrument signed by Purchaser and Seller or, in the case of a waiver, by the party waiving compliance. No delay on the part of any party in exercising any right, power or privilege hereunder shall operate as a waiver thereof; nor shall any waiver on the part of any party of any such right, power or privilege, nor any single or partial exercise of any such right, power or privilege, preclude any further exercise thereof or the exercise of any other such right, power or privilege. The rights and remedies herein provided are cumulative and are not exclusive of any rights or remedies that any party may otherwise have at law or in equity.

Severability. This Agreement shall be deemed severable and the invalidity or unenforceability of any term or provision hereof shall not affect the validity or enforceability of this Agreement or of any other term or provision hereof.

Section Headings. The section headings contained in this Agreement are solely for convenience of reference and shall not affect the meaning or interpretation of this Agreement or of any term or provision hereof.

Counterparts; Terms. This Agreement may be executed in two or more counterparts, each of which shall be deemed an original and all of which together shall be considered one and the same agreement. All references herein to Articles, Sections, Subsections, clauses, Exhibits and Schedules shall be deemed references to such parts of this Agreement, unless the context shall otherwise require. All references to singular or plural or masculine or feminine shall include the other as the context may require.

Governing Law; Consent to Jurisdiction; Venue. This Agreement shall be governed by and construed in accordance with the internal laws (as opposed to conflicts of law provisions) of the State of Missouri.

Exhibits and Schedules. The Exhibits attached hereto are a part of this Agreement as if fully set forth herein. The Schedules referred to herein mean the schedules set forth in that certain letter agreement, of even date herewith, being furnished to Purchaser by Seller.

(Signature pages follow)

IN WITNESS WHEREOF, Purchaser and Seller have caused this Stock Purchase Agreement to be signed as of the date first written above.

SELLER: **PURCHASER:**

_____   _____

_____   _____
John Doe, an Individual

_____
Jane Doe, an Individual

THE COMPANY:

_____
John Doe, President

Employment Agreement Checklist

Term of agreement

Define period of time covered by agreement (and auto renewals, if applicable)

Specify periodic adjustments to compensation, if applicable

Define exit notice requirements, from either side, for termination

Job role

Define title and approximate job role anticipated

Specify requirements for agreement on major change to job role or to job location

Compensation

Define base salary payments required, and timing for payment

Define any bonus arrangements to be predetermined, with attention to clarity on mechanisms for computation and payment timing; also, if complex, consider definition of dispute resolution mechanism

Benefits

Specify inclusion in core benefit package for company

Detail any significant special benefits or perks to be included

If company car is to be provided, outline requirements and specify any buy-out privileges upon termination

Noncompete

Specify duration of any noncompete provisions post employment, and likewise for confidentiality, if appropriate; also geographic range, if appropriate

Clearly define what is competition (limit to competition with company as operated during employee's tenure)

If appropriate, specify restrictions on hiring of staff from company, post employment

Change of control clause

Impact upon term of employment commitment

Termination benefits, if applicable

Stay bonus, if applicable

Shareholder Agreement Checklist

(1) Protections for Company

Agreements generally need some sort of buy-back mechanism for minority shareholder heirs, or for shareholder employees if stock repurchase is preferred when they leave employ of company.

Stock buy-back provisions need to provide for the potential for delayed payment in the event of company financial hardship, or in the event that multiple minority shareholders exit at the same time.

Buy back agreements need some sort of formula pricing, which is pre-defined. (Appraisal mechanisms don't work—too discretionary—value estimates can vary wildly).

Company needs certain fundamental noncompetition and confidentiality provisions for any shareholder. (See also 3 below)

Agreements generally need to provide that minority blocks of stock will not be sold to outsiders and may also need to deal with the potential for limitation of voting rights.

(2) Protections for Shareholder

Shareholder needs repurchase provisions to avoid being held in low-power minority position after involvement in company ceases (important also for heirs).

Shareholder needs protection to insure efforts to remove from any debt guarantees in the event of exit. (Will require bank approval, so will probably have to be replaced by other guarantees or security interests.)

Shareholder should review by-laws to be familiar with rights and voting dynamics.

Shareholder may want "resale protection" or "clawback provision" to provide that if stock repurchased from him is in turn sold for large profit within a predefined period of time he will share to some degree in such profit (common provisions are 50% recapture of "lost profit" if sale occurs within a year, declining rapidly for a period of two or three years post sale);

(3) Noncompetes/Confidentiality

Shareholders should generally have some noncompete, which will survive sale for a period of at least two to three years. This applies to employee shareholders certainly, but often even to outside private investors.

Noncompetes should include a "no hire" provision for shareholders regarding company personnel.

Generally should include a trade secrets provision, which would prohibit sharing of confidential data.

Often agreements would restrict ownership of or employment by a competitor.

The agreement may provide for "peaceable sale" provision, requiring cooperative behavior in courting sale, reasonable transition to buyer and at least minimal post-sale employment (perhaps one year, but would often also provide pay for one year "parachute" payment if new buyer didn't want the given shareholder-employee.)

(4) Buy/Sell Mechanisms

Formula pricing is simplest, and least subject to dispute. Typical formula might provide for value set at four to five times EBIT, less debt. If earnings are low, formula might provide book value price, if that's greater. Consider void of any purchase commitment if company is losing more than five percent of sales. If using formula with average earnings, should be heavily weighted to most recent year.

Consider possible put/call provision, allowing one shareholder to make an offer to another, where the other must either accept that offer or beat it by some specified dollar amount within 30–90 days (shorter time period is better if possible, because efforts to raise support capital can be very distracting from operation. Also, any proposal to buy should be accompanied by a substantial nonrefundable deposit, to insure good faith intent to close.)

Another possible mechanism would include an "insider auction provision", where shareholders agree to a cross-auction at some specified future date. (Generally, might be 60–90 days out. This gives time for preparation in advance, so that shareholders can do adequate due diligence to allow them to know how much they can bid. Again, winning shareholder should make sizable deposit.)

The "Suicide" provision is another fast and highly decisive mechanism, which tends to avoid frivolous discussions of sale. Any shareholder is permitted to put forth an offer to purchase at his estimated value pricing, generally with a simultaneous deposit to indicate certainty of financial capability and commitment to carry through. The other shareholder then can either accept such offer, or decline it, and instead pay the same price to the would-be buyer. Generally some reasonable fixed time period must be allowed for response, and the response, if to buy instead of sell, must be accompanied by a like deposit.

(5) Guarantees of Company Debt

If more than one shareholder guarantee is required on debt, bank will likely require "joint and several" responsibility. Because this means that bank can call for guarantee service by easiest or wealthiest party, each shareholder should maintain the right for reimbursement by other shareholders, with all legal protections possible.

If guarantees are called, consider agreements to provide for key assets or secondary asset collateral rights to go to shareholder who paid on guarantee, to help ensure recovery of forfeited amounts. Also, consider provision to ratchet up ownership in such event.

(6) Company Debt to Shareholders

If shareholders loan amounts to company, collateral should be provided, if possible (even secondary positions on collateral are worthwhile.).

Consider provisions for convertibility to stock, if payment provisions are not met.

Consider operating restrictions if timely repayments are not made.

Provide for periodic financial information to lender-shareholder.

(7) Shareholder Debt to Company

Shareholders borrowing from company should pledge assets as collateral if possible (even insufficient assets, if important to shareholder, can provide important security.)

Require spouse's co-signature on any debt (can be important to protection of rights, to avoid circumvention by transfer of assets to spouse.)

Be alert to and concerned about significant shareholder assets in Florida, Texas, or other states especially favorable to debtors.

(8) Operating Restrictions

Consider requirement for all shareholder concurrence on certain major events (major capital expenditures, major new debt, major asset disposals, Chapter 11 filing, etc.).

Consider requirements for noncompetes to be mandatory for all people hired or promoted to certain key positions.

Consider hiring restrictions for family members.

Consider restrictions against operating asset diversion (for use in other business endeavors), or consider promise of prorata participation in related side ventures.

Consider arbitration clause to resolve by third party any disputes about operating restrictions (generally arbitration works better for operating restriction disputes than for financial or value issues).

(9) Assets Outside of the Company

Provide for continued asset utilization at fair market value for any personal shareholder assets leased or loaned to the company, in the event of shareholder exit.

Provide for reasonable transition and/or temporary access in the event that a personal asset used by the company is to be sold by the individual shareholder.

Appendix IX

Value Enhancement Checklist

I
OVERALL SALABILITY

Perform periodic (we suggest quarterly) analysis of approximate value levels of the company, based on a simple multiple of pretax earnings calculation; seek outside expert advice for comparative multiples common in your industry.

Develop a file of press clippings with historical information about related industry buy or sell transactions which have occurred in recent times.

Build a press file with clippings on company progress, awards, and newsworthy events.

Develop a listing of all intangible assets owned, and use such listing as a checklist to ensure keeping patents, copyrights, license agreements, or any other assets of this sort current and up-to-date.

Prepare at least an annual SWOT analysis—Strengths, Weaknesses, Opportunities, and Threats, and utilize information gleaned to enhance action plans for the coming year.

Review compliance history with ERISA, the IRS, and with Sales and other tax authorities, with focused attention upon "cleaning up" any pending issues or risk areas.

II
FINANCIAL

Develop solid and steadily improving targets for prime financial objectives, including:

- Pretax earnings, as a percentage of sales
- Sales growth, as a percentage, per year
- Gross profit margins
- Debt levels (object here is declining)

Plan to "clean up" all balance sheet items, writing off any unusable or non-salable items on the balance sheet, and making sure all liabilities are reasonably and conservatively stated.

Prepare an annual budget of planned financial performance, and become accustomed to utilizing this tool to site any problems or changes which might require attention.

Obtain any available key financial statistics from others in your industry, and compare and analyze your reports relative to other norms, to both know your strengths, and to monitor and correct potential deficiencies.

Evaluate and enhance financial reporting systems, to ensure, **(a)** timely and quick internal statement availability (preferably within 7–10 days of each month end), **(b)** minimal "audit" or review adjustments at the end of each fiscal year, **(c)** reliable and well-policed inventories of all active and current contractual commitments, **(d)** regular monthly compliance checks to ensure adherence to all loan covenants, and **(e)** up-to-date corporate minutes.

III
MARKETING AND SALES

Develop quality hard copy brochures of products or projects being sold.

Develop a photo file of products or processes successfully completed.

Consider a customer satisfaction survey, to document results, and to provide feedback for any areas needing remedial attention.

Track sales order backlogs, or prospective sales lead inventories regularly, and begin to monitor year-to-date trends of such prospect or backlog reports to same reports from prior years.

Analyze top customers with > 5% of company volume, and work on long term sales contracts, special services, or other mechanisms you might develop to solidify such relationships.

If you use dealers or reps for sales efforts, periodically do an evaluation of quality and range, and develop a long term plan for continuous enhancement of network.

Develop a positive PR plan within your industry, to build reputation.

IV
PEOPLE

Assess organizational management strengths, and target development of at least two tiers of potential leadership within each major area; try to ensure that no single individual manager has direct report responsibility for more than 6 individuals (except at the lowest and simplest levels).

Consider implementing a policy with noncompetes for people in management posts, and confidentiality requirements with secrecy agreements for anyone who deals in proprietary confidential information.

Build a plan to ensure key customer contact with more than one person in the organization.

Inventory your management strengths, with special attention to anyone 55 or older, to ensure you have identified potential developing people as potential future replacements.

V
PROPERTY AND EQUIPMENT

Build a photo file with clear quality photographs of all facilities. If possible also maintain blueprints or floorplans of all key facilities.

Consider an appraisal of real property owned by the company or by related parties.

Consider equipment appraisals, and/or equipment replacement cost analyses for files.

Take "outsider" look at plant and offices, to ascertain clean up needed well ahead of prospective buyer visits.

Assess any compliance issues with OSHA, EPA, water, sewer, or clean air authorities (if applicable), or other governmental agencies or authorities. Develop plans to move to a clean bill of health in all areas in advance of sale.

Consider a Phase I environmental review, if you have never had one done.

Index